MW01630033

fresh and simple™

quick-toss salad meals

BARNES & NOBLE BOOKS

NEW YORK

Previously published as
Better Homes and Gardens® Fresh and Simple™ Quick-Toss Salad Meals

Copyright © 2004, 1998 by Meredith Corporation, Des Moines, Iowa. First Edition.

This edition published for Barnes & Noble, Inc., by Meredith Books.

Printed in China

ISBN: 0-7607-6024-1

contents

salads are for supper

Mom always told you to eat your greens. She never imagined that salads would grow up, too. They now are complete meals, full of flavor and personality. Innovations in packaged greens and a dramatic increase in fresh produce offerings make these meals a breeze to prepare. Even with time at a premium, you can eat wisely and well. Healthful and alluring, *Quick-Toss Salad Meals* offers a tempting variety of colors, textures, and tastes. So get fresh. Your mom would approve.

mixed
grill

spicy steak & ranch salad

Steak and onions as you've never seen them before! Grilled sirloin is perked up by Cajun spices before slicing, then arranged on tossed greens and topped with a scattering of crispy French-fried onions. This new version has the makings of an instant classic.

Start to finish: 25 minutes   Makes 4 servings

In a large nonstick skillet cook French-fried onions over medium-high heat about 2 minutes or until browned, stirring occasionally. Set aside.

Meanwhile, combine Cajun seasoning, lime juice, and garlic; rub over both sides of steak. In the same skillet cook steak over medium heat to desired doneness, turning once. (Allow 6 to 8 minutes for medium rare or 9 to 12 minutes for medium.) Remove skillet from heat; let stand for 10 minutes. Cut steak into thin bite-size slices. If desired, season with salt.

On a large serving platter toss together the salad greens, carrots, and radishes. Arrange steak strips over salad greens. Drizzle dressing over salad. Sprinkle with onions.

Nutrition facts per serving: 310 cal., 13 g total fat (4 g sat. fat), 76 mg chol., 557 mg sodium, 16 g carbo., 3 g fiber, 28 g pro. Daily values: 126% vit. A, 40% vit. C, 5% calcium, 28% iron

½ cup French-fried onions

1 tablespoon Cajun seasoning

1 tablespoon lime juice

1 clove garlic, minced

1 pound boneless beef top sirloin steak, cut 1 inch thick

1 10-ounce package European-style salad greens

2 carrots, cut into thin bite-size strips or peeled into thin strips

½ cup thinly sliced radishes

½ cup bottled fat-free ranch salad dressing

beef & beet salad with fresh basil dressing

It's amazing. Eaters who shy away from cooked vegetables are ever-so-adventurous when the veggies are served cool and crisp in a salad. Case in point is this mélange of sliced beets, carrots, parsnips, and zucchini, fortified with lean strips of beef.

6 cups torn mixed salad greens

½ pound lean cooked beef, cut into thin bite-size strips

1 small parsnip, thinly sliced (½ cup)

1 medium carrot, thinly sliced (½ cup)

½ cup sliced zucchini

1 recipe Fresh Basil Dressing

½ of a 16-ounce can (about ¾ cup) julienned beets, well drained

Start to finish: 25 minutes   Makes 4 servings

In a large bowl toss together salad greens, beef strips, parsnip, carrot, and zucchini. Pour dressing over salad. Toss lightly to coat. Top with beets.

Fresh Basil Dressing: In a small bowl gradually stir ¼ cup buttermilk into ¼ cup mayonnaise or salad dressing. Stir in 1 tablespoon snipped fresh basil or ½ teaspoon dried basil, crushed, and dash pepper.

Nutrition facts per serving: 258 cal., 15 g total fat (3 g sat. fat), 41 mg chol., 245 mg sodium, 11 g carbo., 3 g fiber, 20 g pro. Daily values: 55% vit. A, 26% vit. C, 5% calcium, 20% iron

cooking with **fresh beets**

Fresh beets from the garden or farmer's market can be successfully substituted for canned with a little extra preparation. Wash the beets, slice off the roots and tops, leaving 1 inch of stem. Then cook, covered, in boiling water for 40 to 50 minutes or until tender. Drain and cool slightly. Peel off the skins and julienne or slice.

grilled steak & potato salad

Warm cubes of grilled steak and new potatoes, laced with Dijon-style mustard, provide a satisfying contrast to cool lettuce leaves in this do-on-the-grill dinner.

Prep: 15 minutes   Grill: 35 minutes   Makes 4 servings

Place potatoes and water in a foil packet, leaving space for steam to build. Grill potato packet on the rack of an uncovered grill directly over medium coals for 20 minutes. Turn packet over; grill about 15 minutes more or until potatoes are tender.

Add steak to grill when potato packet is turned; grill over medium coals to desired doneness, turning once. (Allow 8 to 12 minutes for medium-rare and 12 to 15 minutes for medium.) Spread steak with 1 tablespoon of the mustard blend during the last 5 minutes of grilling. Remove steak and potato packet from grill; let stand while preparing dressing.

For dressing, in a large bowl combine the remaining 2 tablespoons of the mustard blend, the onion or ranch dip, milk, Worcestershire sauce, and pepper. Drain potatoes and add to dressing; toss lightly to coat. Cut steak into thin bite-size slices.

Line 4 plates with lettuce leaves. Arrange steak slices on lettuce-lined plates. Top each with potatoes and green onions.

Nutrition facts per serving: 375 cal., 13 g total fat (4 g sat. fat), 50 mg chol., 346 mg sodium, 42 g carbo., 2 g fiber, 22 g pro. Daily values: 2% vit. A, 41% vit. C, 3% calcium, 30% iron

1½ **pounds whole tiny new potatoes, quartered**

¼ **cup water**

12 **ounces beef rib-eye steak or beef top sirloin steak, cut 1 inch thick**

3 **tablespoons creamy Dijon-style mustard blend**

¼ **cup dairy sour cream onion or ranch dip**

1 **tablespoon milk**

½ **teaspoon Worcestershire sauce**

⅛ **teaspoon pepper**

  Lettuce leaves

2 **green onions, thinly sliced**

steak salad

Turn leftover steak into a spectacular second-day salad that wakes taste buds with red onion, blue cheese, and tarragon dressing. Or, fire up the grill and enjoy the pairing of warm steak with cool, buttery Boston lettuce.

½ cup bottled light red wine vinegar and oil salad dressing

1 tablespoon snipped fresh tarragon or ½ to 1 teaspoon dried tarragon, crushed

½ teaspoon cracked or coarsely ground pepper

2 heads Boston lettuce, separated into leaves

½ pound lean cooked beef, cut into thin bite-size strips

1 cup red or yellow baby pear tomatoes

1 cup broccoli flowerets

½ of a medium red onion, cut into thin slices

¼ cup crumbled blue cheese (1 ounce)

½ cup fat-free croutons

Start to finish: 25 minutes   Makes 4 servings

For dressing, combine salad dressing, tarragon, and pepper; set aside.

Line 4 plates with lettuce leaves. Arrange beef, tomatoes, broccoli, and onion on plates. Sprinkle with blue cheese. Drizzle with dressing and top with croutons.

Nutrition facts per serving: 229 cal., 11 g total fat (3 g sat. fat), 42 mg chol., 497 mg sodium, 12 g carbo., 3 g fiber, 21 g pro. Daily values: 16% vit. A, 65% vit. C, 7% calcium, 15% iron

philly-style
cheese-steak salad

Cheese steaks are hometown nostalgia fare. Re-create the sweet smell of onions and peppers on the grill, toss them with sirloin strips and a cheesy dressing, and you'll swear you can hear do-wop on the corner.

Start to finish: 30 minutes   Makes 4 servings

For pita chips, split pita rounds horizontally to make 4 rounds; cut each into 6 wedges. Place on a foil-lined baking sheet. Bake in 350° oven for 8 to 10 minutes or until crisp. Sprinkle with shredded cheese; bake 2 to 3 minutes more or until cheese melts. Set chips aside.

For dressing, in a blender container or food processor bowl, combine salad dressing and semisoft cheese. Cover and blend or process until smooth. Add milk, 1 tablespoon at a time, to make desired consistency. Set dressing aside.

In a large skillet cook sweet pepper strips and onion in hot oil about 4 minutes or until crisp-tender. Remove from skillet. In the same skillet, cook beef strips over medium-high heat for 2 to 3 minutes or until desired doneness. (Add more oil, if necessary.) Return sweet pepper strips and onion to the skillet, stirring to combine; heat through.

On a large serving platter toss together hot beef mixture and salad greens. Drizzle dressing over salad. Serve with pita chips.

Nutrition facts per serving: 457 cal., 23 g total fat (11 g sat. fat), 74 mg chol., 743 mg sodium, 30 g carbo., 2 g fiber, 30 g pro. Daily values: 28% vit. A, 125% vit. C, 16% calcium, 24% iron

2	pita bread rounds
¾	cup shredded Italian-blend cheeses (3 ounces)
½	cup bottled fat-free creamy peppercorn ranch salad dressing
¼	cup semisoft cheese with garlic and herb
	Milk
1	red sweet pepper, cut into thin strips
1	yellow sweet pepper, cut into thin strips
1	small onion, cut into thin wedges
1	to 2 tablespoons olive oil
12	ounces boneless beef top sirloin steak, cut into thin bite-size strips
8	cups torn mixed salad greens

beef & apple salad

Meal appeal comes from taste, aroma, presentation, and texture, an under-appreciated element that adds snap to a dish. This crunchy example includes crisp raw apples, jicama, and carrots, along with slices of beef.

Start to finish: 30 minutes   Makes 4 servings

For dressing, in a screw-top jar combine apple juice, salad oil, and vinegar. Cover and shake well.

Line 4 plates with lettuce leaves. Arrange the apples, beef, jicama, and carrots atop lettuce. Top with cherries. Drizzle dressing over salads. If desired, sprinkle with pepper.

Nutrition facts per serving: 327 cal., 18 g total fat (4 g sat. fat), 33 mg chol., 62 mg sodium, 25 g carbo., 3 g fiber, 19 g pro. Daily values: 106% vit. A, 34% vit. C, 2% calcium, 16% iron

¼ cup apple juice

¼ cup salad oil

2 tablespoons wine vinegar

Lettuce leaves

2 medium apples or pears, cut into wedges

8 ounces lean cooked beef, cut into thin bite-size strips (1½ cups)

1 cup jicama cut into thin bite-size strips

2 medium carrots, cut into thin bite-size strips (1 cup)

¼ cup dried cherries or cranberries, snipped

Coarsely ground pepper (optional)

beef & curry pinwheels on spinach

Pick up roast beef sliced to your liking at the deli, and the work is half done for this protein-rich entrée. Fresh asparagus is a crisp counterpoint to the curry and chutney cream filling that's spread on the beef slices.

1 pound asparagus spears

⅓ of an 8-ounce tub (about ⅓ cup) cream cheese

3 tablespoons peach or mango chutney, snipped

2 tablespoons finely chopped green onion

¼ teaspoon curry powder

½ pound lean cooked beef, thinly sliced (about 8 slices)

6 cups torn fresh spinach or torn mixed salad greens

2 tablespoons lemon juice

1 tablespoon olive oil

2 tablespoons chopped peanuts

Start to finish: 30 minutes   Makes 4 servings

Snap off and discard woody bases from asparagus. Cook asparagus spears, covered, in a small amount of boiling water for 4 to 6 minutes or until crisp-tender. Drain; set aside.

Meanwhile, in a small bowl stir together cream cheese, chutney, green onion, and curry powder. Spread about 1 tablespoon of the cream cheese mixture over each beef slice. Roll up each beef slice, starting from the short side; cut each beef pinwheel in half.

Divide spinach among 4 plates. Arrange asparagus spears atop spinach. Stir together the lemon juice and olive oil; drizzle over spinach and asparagus. Arrange 4 of the beef pinwheels on each plate; sprinkle with the peanuts.

Nutrition facts per serving: 317 cal., 19 g total fat (6 g sat. fat), 71 mg chol., 213 mg sodium, 16 g carbo., 4 g fiber, 24 g pro. Daily values: 66% vit. A, 76% vit. C, 10% calcium, 31% iron

pork & pear spinach salad

Fruit, cheese, and nuts are a classic trio with endless intriguing combinations. When you introduce them to savory onions and pork, and dress them all with a mustard-vinegar topping, you have a salad for the ages.

15

Start to finish: 25 minutes   Makes 3 servings

Divide spinach among 3 plates. Arrange pear, pork, and onion on the spinach. Sprinkle with cheese and nuts. Drizzle dressing over salads.

Mustard Dressing: In a screw-top jar combine 2 tablespoons olive oil or salad oil, 2 tablespoons vinegar or white wine vinegar, 1½ teaspoons sugar, ¼ teaspoon celery seed, and ⅛ teaspoon dry mustard or ½ teaspoon Dijon-style mustard. Cover and shake well.

Nutrition facts per serving: 331 cal., 22 g total fat (6 g sat. fat), 57 mg chol., 155 mg sodium, 16 g carbo., 4 g fiber, 20 g pro. Daily values: 52% vit. A, 40% vit. C, 9% calcium, 20% iron

Note: To toast a small amount of nuts, place them in a small skillet. Cook over medium heat, stirring often, for 5 to 7 minutes or until golden.

4 cups torn fresh spinach

1 medium pear or apple, cored and sliced, or 1½ cups red or green seedless grapes

1 cup cooked lean pork or beef cut into thin strips

½ of a small red or white onion, thinly sliced and separated into rings

1 ounce Brie cheese, cut into thin wedges or cubes, or ¼ cup crumbled blue cheese or feta cheese (1 ounce)

2 tablespoons broken walnuts or pecans or slivered almonds, toasted*

1 recipe Mustard Dressing

thai cobb salad

Hit a home run with this refreshing mix of meat, cubed avocado, roasted peanuts, and spicy ginger-soy dressing. Leftover grilled meats work admirably, or deli-sliced meats can pinch-hit.

16

½ cup bottled fat-free Italian salad
    dressing

1 tablespoon soy sauce

1 to 1½ teaspoons grated gingerroot

¼ to ½ teaspoon crushed red pepper

8 cups torn mixed salad greens*

1½ cups coarsely chopped cooked
    pork, beef, or chicken
    (8 ounces)

1 avocado, halved, seeded, peeled,
    and cut into ½-inch pieces

1 cup coarsely shredded carrots

¼ cup fresh cilantro leaves

¼ cup thinly sliced green onions

¼ cup honey-roasted peanuts
    (optional)

Start to finish: 25 minutes   Makes 4 servings

For dressing, in a large bowl combine dressing, soy sauce, gingerroot, and crushed red pepper. Add salad greens; toss lightly to coat.

Divide salad greens among 4 plates. Top each with meat, avocado, carrots, cilantro, green onions, and, if desired, peanuts.

Nutrition facts per serving: 255 cal., 15 g total fat (4 g sat. fat), 52 mg chol., 743 mg sodium, 11 g carbo., 4 g fiber, 19 g pro. Daily values: 86% vit. A, 19% vit. C, 3% calcium, 13% iron

Note: To carry through with the Asian flavors, include Chinese cabbage as part of the mixed greens.

storing and **using fresh ginger**

Whole gingerroot stays fresh for two or three weeks in the refrigerator when wrapped loosely in a paper towel, and lasts almost indefinitely when frozen. To freeze, place unpeeled gingerroot in a freezer bag. You can grate or slice the ginger while it's frozen.

pork salad
with **cabbage** slaw

Apples and pork are a can't-miss combination, so this entrée repeats it twice: chopped apples with sliced pork loin and cider vinegar with crumbled bacon. It's a good change of pace, made easy with a base of packaged coleslaw mix.

1 **pound butterflied pork loin chops, cut about ¾ inch thick**

¼ **teaspoon cracked black pepper**

⅛ **teaspoon ground nutmeg**

5 **cups packaged shredded cabbage with carrot (coleslaw mix)**

1 **large apple, coarsely chopped**

2 **slices turkey bacon or bacon**

⅓ **cup cider vinegar**

⅓ **cup apple juice or apple cider**

1 **tablespoon honey**

2 **teaspoons honey mustard**

1 **teaspoon caraway seed**

Start to finish: 30 minutes   Makes 4 servings

Sprinkle chops with pepper and nutmeg. Place on the unheated rack of a broiler pan. Broil 4 to 5 inches from heat for 12 to 15 minutes or until juices run clear and no pink remains, turning once.

Meanwhile, in a large bowl combine cabbage and apple; set aside. Cook bacon in a medium skillet until crisp. Drain; crumble and set aside.

Stir vinegar, apple juice, honey, honey mustard, and caraway seed into skillet. Bring to boiling. Pour over cabbage mixture; add bacon. Toss lightly to coat.

Divide cabbage mixture among 4 plates. Cut chops into ¼-inch-thick slices. Arrange pork slices atop cabbage mixture.

Nutrition facts per serving: 235 cal., 9 g total fat (3 g sat. fat), 56 mg chol., 171 mg sodium, 21 g carbo., 3 g fiber, 19 g pro. Daily values: 78% vit. A, 78% vit. C, 5% calcium, 11% iron

spinach, ham, & melon salad

Start to finish: 30 minutes   Makes 4 servings

Use a melon baller to scoop out the cantaloupe pulp into balls.

In a large bowl toss together cantaloupe balls, spinach, ham, pecans, and red onion slices. Pour dressing over salad. Toss lightly to coat.

Orange-Poppy Seed Dressing: In a food processor bowl or blender container, combine 3 tablespoons sugar, 1½ teaspoons finely shredded orange peel, 2 tablespoons orange juice, 2 tablespoons vinegar, 1 tablespoon finely chopped onion, and dash pepper. Cover and process or blend until combined. With processor or blender running, slowly add ⅓ cup salad oil in a steady stream through hole or opening in top. Process or blend until mixture is thickened. Stir in 1 teaspoon poppy seed. Cover and chill for up to 1 week. Shake well before using. Makes about ¾ cup.

Nutrition facts per serving: 286 cal., 20 g total fat (3 g sat. fat), 19 mg chol., 507 mg sodium, 19 g carbo., 4 g fiber, 12 g pro. Daily values: 91% vit. A, 119% vit. C, 10% calcium, 24% iron

½ of a small cantaloupe

7 cups torn fresh spinach

1 cup cubed cooked lean ham

½ cup pecan halves, toasted

½ of a medium red onion, thinly sliced

⅓ cup Orange-Poppy Seed Dressing

BLT salad with crostini

BLTs have been a part of the American food experience for decades, but crostini, savory grilled bread slices topped with tomato and garlic, is a more recent addition to our dining vocabulary and an inspired sidekick to the legendary combo.

Start to finish: 30 minutes   Makes 4 servings

For dressing, in a blender container or food processor bowl, combine mayonnaise or salad dressing, milk, dried tomatoes, and garlic. Cover and blend or process until tomatoes and garlic are finely chopped. Set dressing aside.

Place bread slices on a baking sheet. Bake in a 450° oven for about 5 minutes or until toasted. Turn slices over; spread with some of the dressing. Bake 3 minutes more; set aside.

Meanwhile, in a large bowl toss together salad greens, chopped tomato, cucumber, cheese, and bacon. Drizzle with dressing; toss lightly to coat. Serve with toasted bread slices.

Nutrition facts per serving: 236 cal., 12 g total fat (5 g sat. fat), 33 mg chol., 913 mg sodium, 22 g carbo., 2 g fiber, 13 g pro. Daily values: 12% vit. A, 31% vit. C, 14% calcium, 10% iron

⅓ **cup fat-free mayonnaise dressing or salad dressing**

4 **tablespoons milk**

2 **tablespoons chopped oil-packed dried tomatoes, drained**

1 **clove garlic, minced**

12 **thin slices baguette-style French bread**

6 **cups torn mixed salad greens**

3 **plum tomatoes, seeded and chopped (1 cup)**

1 **small cucumber, halved lengthwise and thinly sliced**

½ **cup cubed Muenster or mozzarella cheese (2 ounces)**

8 **slices turkey bacon, crisp-cooked, drained, and crumbled**

pizza in a bowl

Bread salads are an old-world tradition, updated here to reflect our long love affair with pizza. Premade pizza crusts and packaged salad greens make the prep work child's play: Open packages and toss.

¾ **cup bottled fat-free Western or French salad dressing**

1 **tablespoon snipped fresh basil or oregano or ½ teaspoon dried basil or oregano, crushed**

8 **cups torn romaine**

1 **8-ounce package (2) Italian bread shells (Boboli), torn into bite-size pieces**

1 **cup chopped Canadian-style bacon or pepperoni**

1 **cup shredded reduced-fat mozzarella cheese or pizza cheese (4 ounces)**

Start to finish: 20 minutes   Makes 4 servings

For dressing, in a small bowl combine salad dressing and basil or oregano; set aside.

In an extra-large bowl toss together romaine, bread shells, meat, and cheese. Drizzle with dressing; toss lightly to coat.

Nutrition facts per serving: 341 cal., 10 g total fat (1 g sat. fat), 33 mg chol., 1,375 mg sodium, 38 g carbo., 3 g fiber, 25 g pro. Daily values: 47% vit. A, 57% vit. C, 8% calcium, 17% iron

balsamic-glazed
springtime lamb salad

Balsamic vinegar, a less-astringent, sweeter member of the vinegar family, makes a memorable glaze for grilled lamb chops. Add fresh early pea pods and mixed greens, and the dish defines the essence of spring.

Start to finish: 25 minutes   Makes 4 servings

For glaze, in a small saucepan bring balsamic vinegar just to boiling. Boil gently, uncovered, about 10 minutes or until vinegar is reduced to ⅓ cup. Set glaze aside.

Meanwhile, place chops on the unheated rack of a broiler pan. Broil 3 to 4 inches from heat for 7 to 11 minutes for medium doneness, turning once halfway through.

Cook peas, covered, in a small amount of boiling salted water for 2 to 4 minutes or until crisp-tender. Drain.

Divide salad greens among 4 plates. Top each with 2 lamb chops and some of the sugar snap peas. Drizzle with glaze; sprinkle with nuts.

Nutrition facts per serving: 516 cal., 21 g total fat (6 g sat. fat), 160 mg chol., 163 mg sodium, 23 g carbo., 4 g fiber, 55 g pro. Daily values: 3% vit. A, 85% vit. C, 7% calcium, 51% iron

1   cup balsamic vinegar

8   lamb loin or rib chops, cut
    1 inch thick

3   cups sugar snap peas, ends
    trimmed

6   cups torn mixed salad greens

¼   cup hazelnuts or coarsely
    chopped walnuts, toasted

greek lamb salad with yogurt dressing

When menus become ho-hum, bring drama to the table with the elemental Greek trio of lamb, yogurt, and cucumber. Dried tart cherries make the dish sparkle.

24

2	teaspoons snipped fresh rosemary or ½ teaspoon dried rosemary, crushed
1	clove garlic, minced
8	ounces boneless lamb leg sirloin chops, cut ½ inch thick
8	cups torn fresh spinach or torn mixed salad greens
1	15-ounce can garbanzo beans, rinsed and drained
¼	cup chopped, seeded cucumber
½	cup plain low-fat yogurt
¼	cup chopped green onions
⅛	to ¼ teaspoon salt
⅛	teaspoon pepper
1	clove garlic, minced
¼	cup dried tart cherries or golden raisins

Start to finish: 30 minutes   Makes 4 servings

Combine rosemary and 1 clove garlic; rub evenly onto lamb chops. Place chops on the unheated rack of a broiler pan. Broil 4 to 5 inches from the heat for 12 to 15 minutes, turning once halfway through.* Cut lamb chops into thin bite-size slices.

Meanwhile, in a large bowl toss together spinach, garbanzo beans, and cucumber. Divide spinach mixture among 4 plates. Arrange lamb slices atop spinach mixture.

For dressing, in a small bowl combine yogurt, green onions, salt, pepper, and 1 clove garlic. Drizzle dressing over salads. Sprinkle with cherries.

Nutrition facts per serving: 243 cal., 6 g total fat (2 g sat. fat), 36 mg chol., 569 mg sodium, 29 g carbo., 8 g fiber, 20 g pro. Daily values: 80% vit. A, 63% vit. C, 17% calcium, 42% iron

Note: If desired, grill chops on the rack of an uncovered grill directly over medium coals to desired doneness, turning once halfway through. (Allow 10 to 14 minutes for medium-rare or 14 to 16 minutes for medium.)

chicken salad
grows up

strawberry-peppercorn
vinaigrette with turkey

An enduring combination is the mix of hot and sweet. See what the fuss is about with a dressing that combines sweet strawberries and pungent cracked pepper. It gives chicken salad a wake-up call.

Start to finish: 25 minutes   Makes 4 servings

Divide mesclun among 4 plates. Top each with turkey, kiwifruit, mushrooms, and tomatoes. Drizzle vinaigrette over salads. Toss lightly to coat.

Strawberry-Peppercorn Vinaigrette: In a food processor bowl or blender container, combine 1 cup cut-up fresh or frozen strawberries (thaw frozen strawberries), 2 tablespoons red wine vinegar, and $\frac{1}{8}$ teaspoon cracked black pepper. Cover and process or blend until smooth.

Nutrition facts per serving: 251 cal., 8 g total fat (2 g sat. fat), 84 mg chol., 102 mg sodium, 15 g carbo., 5 g fiber, 31 g pro. Daily values: 32% vit. A, 150% vit. C, 21% iron

8 cups mesclun or 6 cups torn romaine and 2 cups torn curly endive, chicory, or escarole

2½ cups cooked turkey or chicken, cut into bite-size strips (12 ounces)

2 cups sliced, peeled kiwifruit and/or sliced carambola (star fruit)

1½ cups enoki mushrooms (3 ounces)

1 cup red cherry tomatoes and/or yellow baby pear tomatoes, halved

1 recipe Strawberry-Peppercorn Vinaigrette

chicken & pears
with pecan goat cheese

Goat cheese, also known as chèvre, is a popular selection at the cheese shop, thanks to its distinctive tang that plays so well against fruit, nuts, and the bouquet of garden greens known as mesclun. This salad has them all, plus slices of juicy grilled chicken.

8 ounces skinless, boneless chicken breast halves

¼ cup olive oil or salad oil

2 tablespoons balsamic vinegar

¼ teaspoon salt

¼ teaspoon pepper

1 clove garlic, minced

¼ cup finely chopped pecans, toasted

1 4-ounce log semisoft goat cheese (chèvre), cut into ¼-inch-thick slices

8 cups mesclun

2 medium pears or apples, thinly sliced

Start to finish: 30 minutes   Makes 4 servings

Rinse chicken; pat dry. Place chicken on the unheated rack of a broiler pan. Broil 4 to 5 inches from heat about 9 minutes or until no longer pink, turning once.* Cut chicken breasts diagonally into thin slices.

Meanwhile, for dressing, in a screw-top jar combine oil, vinegar, salt, pepper, and garlic. Cover and shake well; set aside. Press toasted pecans onto one side of each cheese slice.

Divide mesclun among 4 plates. Arrange chicken, pears, and cheese atop mesclun. Drizzle with dressing.

Nutrition facts per serving: 389 cal., 28 g total fat (7 g sat. fat), 55 mg chol., 337 mg sodium, 18 g carbo., 4 g fiber, 18 g pro. Daily values: 7% vit. A, 15% vit. C, 5% calcium, 12% iron

Note: If desired, grill chicken on the rack of an uncovered grill directly over medium coals for 12 to 15 minutes or until no longer pink, turning once halfway through.

grilled chicken & raspberry salad

Let's face it: Skinless, boneless chicken needs a supporting cast to perk it up. Raspberry vinegar, red onion, and fresh raspberries combine with mixed greens to produce a festive dish that doesn't get by on looks alone.

¼ **cup raspberry vinegar**

3 **tablespoons cooking oil**

½ **teaspoon poppy seed**

¼ **teaspoon salt**

¼ **teaspoon pepper**

1 **pound skinless, boneless chicken breast halves**

6 **cups torn mixed salad greens**

½ **of a small red onion, thinly sliced and separated into rings**

1 **cup raspberries**

Start to finish: 25 minutes   Makes 4 servings

For dressing, in a screw-top jar combine raspberry vinegar, oil, poppy seed, salt, and pepper. Cover and shake well; set aside.

Rinse chicken; pat dry. Grill chicken on the rack of an uncovered grill directly over medium coals for 12 to 15 minutes or until no longer pink, turning once halfway through. (Or, place chicken on the unheated rack of a broiler pan. Broil 4 to 5 inches from heat about 9 minutes or until no longer pink, turning once.) Cut chicken diagonally into thin slices.

On a large serving platter, arrange salad greens, onion, and chicken. Drizzle with dressing. Sprinkle raspberries over salad.

Nutrition facts per serving: 244 cal., 14 g total fat (2 g sat. fat), 59 mg chol., 190 mg sodium, 8 g carbo., 2 g fiber, 23 g pro. Daily values: 3% vit. A, 19% vit. C, 3% calcium, 10% iron

pasta with
chicken & fruit

Want to bring out the full taste of strawberries? Warm them slightly by mixing with hot pasta, and they'll provide a sweet counterpoint to the tart vinaigrette that dresses crunchy walnuts and chicken strips.

Start to finish: 25 minutes   Makes 4 servings

Cook pasta according to package directions; drain well. Rinse with cold water; drain again.

Place mesclun in a large bowl; add pasta. Toss lightly to combine. Add chicken, strawberries, onion slices, walnuts, and Parmesan cheese. Drizzle with dressing. Toss lightly to coat.

Nutrition facts per serving: 288 cal., 12 g total fat (3 g sat. fat), 39 mg chol., 193 mg sodium, 28 g carbo., 2 g fiber, 19 g pro. Daily values: 4% vit. A, 62% vit. C, 10% calcium, 13% iron

the **mix** of **greens** called **mesclun**

In the Piedmont region of Italy and the neighboring Provence region of France, salads of mixed greens, known as mesclun, have a long and proud tradition. Mesclun is any combination of baby lettuces grown and harvested together that represent a variety of flavors, textures, and colors. Various combinations are classics: A Provençal salad is known for chervil, arugula, and endive. Salad niçoise owes its tangy flavor to chicory, cress, and dandelion greens. Americans have embraced the idea of using diverse greens, and the selection in today's produce sections allows you to create your own intriguing mesclun mixes.

2 cups dried penne

3 cups mesclun or torn fresh spinach

5 ounces cooked chicken, cut into bite-size strips (1 cup)

1 cup sliced strawberries

½ cup sliced red onion

⅓ cup coarsely chopped walnuts, toasted

¼ cup grated Parmesan cheese

½ cup bottled balsamic vinaigrette salad dressing

southwestern chicken & black bean salad

Fusion cooking conquers two continents in this global collaboration of Caesar dressing and a Mexican ingredient list of black beans, tortilla chips, chili powder, and cilantro.

Start to finish: 25 minutes   Makes 4 servings

In a large bowl combine romaine, black beans, chicken, and tomatoes.

For dressing, in a small bowl whisk together salad dressing, chili powder, and cumin. Pour dressing over salad. Toss lightly to coat. Sprinkle with cilantro and tortilla chips.

Nutrition facts per serving: 295 cal., 10 g total fat (1 g sat. fat), 55 mg chol., 913 mg sodium, 26 g carbo., 9 g fiber, 27 g pro. Daily values: 47% vit. A, 83% vit. C, 9% calcium, 30% iron

10 cups torn romaine

1 15-ounce can black beans, rinsed and drained

1½ cups chopped cooked chicken or turkey (about 8 ounces)

1½ cups red and/or yellow cherry tomatoes, halved

½ cup reduced-calorie bottled Caesar salad dressing

2 teaspoons chili powder

½ teaspoon ground cumin

2 tablespoons snipped fresh cilantro or parsley

½ cup broken tortilla chips

cool-as-a-cucumber
chicken salad

The cool in this dish includes its presentation. Shredded chicken surrounds a mound of cubed melon and vegetables, enhanced by a bracing lime-herb dressing. Just the antidote for a sultry day.

34

2 cups cubed cantaloupe and/or honeydew melon

1 cup very finely chopped cucumber

1 cup very finely chopped zucchini

¼ cup thinly sliced green onions

⅓ cup lime juice

2 tablespoons salad oil

2 tablespoons water

2 tablespoons snipped fresh cilantro or mint

1 tablespoon sugar

⅛ teaspoon ground white pepper

4 cups shredded leaf lettuce

2 cups shredded cooked chicken (10 ounces)

Start to finish: 25 minutes   Makes 4 servings

In a large bowl toss together the melon, cucumber, zucchini, and onions.

For dressing, in a screw-top jar combine lime juice, oil, water, cilantro, sugar, and white pepper. Cover and shake well. Drizzle ½ cup of the dressing over the melon mixture. Toss lightly to coat.

Divide lettuce among 4 plates. Top with melon mixture. Arrange chicken around edges of plates. Drizzle remaining dressing over chicken.

Nutrition facts per serving: 268 cal., 13 g total fat (3 g sat. fat), 68 mg chol., 79 mg sodium, 15 g carbo., 2 g fiber, 24 g pro. Daily values: 41% vit. A, 94% vit. C, 6% calcium, 17% iron

poached chicken & pasta
with pesto dressing

What a clever idea: Cut down on pans used in the kitchen by poaching cubed chicken in the same pot with pasta. Once cooked, they're tossed again with a creamy, herb-flecked dressing quickly made with store-bought pesto and sour cream.

Start to finish: 30 minutes   Makes 4 servings

Rinse chicken; pat dry. Cut chicken into 1-inch pieces; set aside.

In a large saucepan cook pasta according to package directions, adding chicken the last 5 to 6 minutes of cooking. Cook until pasta is tender but firm and chicken is no longer pink. Drain pasta and chicken. Rinse with cold water; drain again.

In a large bowl combine pesto and sour cream. Add pasta mixture, chopped vegetables, and tomato. Toss lightly to coat. If desired, sprinkle with nuts.

Nutrition facts per serving: 404 cal., 13 g total fat (1 g sat. fat), 47 mg chol., 183 mg sodium, 43 g carbo., 1 g fiber, 26 g pro. Daily values: 7% vit. A, 61% vit. C, 5% calcium, 15% iron

12	ounces skinless, boneless chicken breast halves
6	ounces dried wagon-wheel macaroni or rotini
¼	cup refrigerated pesto sauce
½	cup fat-free dairy sour cream
1	cup chopped fresh vegetables, such as red, yellow, or green sweet pepper; broccoli flowerets; zucchini; or cucumber
1	small tomato, chopped
¼	cup pine nuts or chopped walnuts, toasted (optional)

sesame chicken kabob salad

Kabobs in a microwave? Yes, indeed. Up-to-the-minute with Asian condiments such as sesame oil and plum sauce, these kabobs have real eye appeal teamed with slender enoki mushrooms and red radishes.

1 pound skinless, boneless chicken breast halves

1 recipe Sesame Dressing

1 tablespoon bottled plum sauce or chili sauce

2 cups chopped red cabbage

2 cups sliced bok choy or iceberg lettuce

16 fresh pineapple wedges

16 sugar snap peas, sliced lengthwise

½ cup enoki mushrooms (1 ounce)

½ cup cut-up radishes

Toasted sesame seed (optional)

Start to finish: 30 minutes   Makes 4 servings

Rinse chicken; pat dry. Cut each chicken breast half lengthwise into 4 strips. Thread 2 of the chicken strips on each of eight 6-inch wooden skewers. Place in a 2-quart rectangular microwave-safe baking dish.

Stir together 2 tablespoons of the dressing and plum sauce; brush over kabobs. Cover dish with waxed paper and microwave on high 2 minutes. Turn kabobs over, rearrange in dish, and brush again with the dressing mixture. Microwave for 2 to 4 minutes more or until chicken is no longer pink.

Meanwhile, combine cabbage and bok choy; divide among 4 plates. Top with kabobs, pineapple, sugar snap peas, mushrooms, and radishes. Drizzle dressing over salads. If desired, sprinkle with sesame seed.

Sesame Dressing: In a screw-top jar combine 3 tablespoons salad oil, 3 tablespoons rice or white wine vinegar, 1 tablespoon toasted sesame oil, 1 tablespoon soy sauce, ½ teaspoon dry mustard, and ¼ teaspoon crushed red pepper. Cover and shake well.

Nutrition facts per serving: 323 cal., 17 g total fat (3 g sat. fat), 59 mg chol., 324 mg sodium, 19 g carbo., 3 g fiber, 24 g pro. Daily values: 6% vit. A, 110% vit. C, 6% calcium, 15% iron

scarlet salad

Beets are such an under-appreciated resource. Give them their due in this variation on a salad niçoise. When beets are combined with colorful asparagus, baby corn, and snow peas, it takes only a little imagination to create stunning arrangements on the plates.

12 ounces whole tiny new potatoes, thinly sliced

12 ounces asparagus spears

6 cups torn mixed salad greens

1½ cups chopped cooked chicken (about 8 ounces)

1 14-ounce can baby corn, drained

1 8-ounce can sliced beets, drained

1 cup fresh snow pea pods, strings and tips removed

⅓ cup chopped red onion

¼ teaspoon cracked black pepper

⅓ cup bottled red wine vinaigrette or other vinaigrette salad dressing

Start to finish: 30 minutes   Makes 4 servings

In a large saucepan cook potatoes, covered, in a small amount of boiling water for 10 minutes. Meanwhile, snap off and discard woody bases from asparagus. Add asparagus spears to saucepan. Cover and cook for 2 to 4 minutes more or until potatoes are tender and asparagus is crisp-tender. Drain. If desired, cover and chill vegetables for up to 24 hours.

To serve, divide salad greens among 4 plates. Arrange the potatoes, asparagus, chicken, baby corn, beets, and snow pea pods atop greens. Sprinkle with chopped onion and pepper. Drizzle dressing over salads.

Nutrition facts per serving: 355 cal., 14 g total fat (3 g sat. fat), 51 mg chol., 574 mg sodium, 34 g carbo., 6 g fiber, 23 g pro. Daily values: 21% vit. A, 107% vit. C, 9% calcium, 34% iron

all **lettuces** are not **created equal**

For those raised on iceberg, lettuce is a mild-mannered ingredient. But the rich array of lettuces and greens on the market these days allows cooks to select varieties for color, and piquant and sweet tastes. Consider compact smooth-textured Bibb, light-green Boston, crunchy loaf-shaped Romaine, and red and green leaf lettuce. They mix nicely with specialty greens such as peppery watercress, tangy arugula, bitter radicchio, and colorful Swiss chard. Prewashed and cut greens, packaged in plastic bags, have expanded our choices and sliced salad preparation time to seconds.

turkey & fruit
with glazed pecans

Glazed nuts are a cook's trump card, because they can be made in advance and saved for a last-minute flourish. Here, sugared pecans mirror the natural sweetness of berries and nectarines, and perk up chunks of broiled turkey tenderloin.

Start to finish: 30 minutes   Makes 4 servings

Rinse turkey; pat dry. Place turkey on the unheated rack of a broiler pan. Broil 4 to 5 inches from the heat for 8 to 10 minutes or until tender and no longer pink, turning once. Cool; cut turkey into bite-size pieces.

In a large bowl toss together turkey, salad greens, nectarines, and strawberries. For dressing, in a small mixing bowl whisk together salad oil, honey, and orange juice. Pour dressing over salad; toss lightly to coat. Sprinkle with pecans.

Glazed Pecans: Place 3 tablespoons sugar in a heavy medium skillet or saucepan. Cook, without stirring, over medium-high heat until the sugar begins to melt, shaking skillet occasionally. Reduce heat to low. Stir with a wooden spoon until sugar is golden brown and completely melted. Add ½ cup pecan halves, stirring to coat. Spread the pecans on buttered foil; cool. Break pecans apart.

Nutrition facts per serving: 425 cal., 22 g total fat (3 g sat. fat), 50 mg chol., 54 mg sodium, 35 g carbo., 4 g fiber, 24 g pro. Daily values: 8% vit. A, 71% vit. C, 3% calcium, 13% iron

1	pound turkey breast tenderloin steaks
6	cups torn mixed salad greens
1½	cups sliced nectarines
1½	cups sliced strawberries
3	tablespoons salad oil
2	tablespoons honey
2	tablespoons orange juice
1	recipe Glazed Pecans

citrusy chicken salad

Brown-skinned jicama tastes like a cross between an apple and a water chestnut. Long used in Mexican cooking, it traverses the globe to add snap to a bright-colored, cumin-flavored salad with Mediterranean credentials.

Start to finish: 25 minutes   Makes 4 servings

For dressing, in a small bowl stir together orange juice concentrate, olive oil, vinegar, cumin, and ground red pepper. Set aside.

In a large bowl toss together salad greens, chicken, oranges, jicama, and sweet pepper. Pour dressing over salad; toss lightly to coat.

Nutrition facts per serving: 348 cal., 20 g total fat (3 g sat. fat), 68 mg chol., 73 mg sodium, 20 g carbo., 2 g fiber, 24 g pro. Daily values: 25% vit. A, 162% vit. C, 4% calcium, 16% iron

⅓ cup frozen orange juice concentrate, thawed

¼ cup olive oil

2 to 3 tablespoons white wine vinegar or white vinegar

1 teaspoon ground cumin

⅛ teaspoon ground red pepper

4 cups torn mixed salad greens

10 ounces cooked chicken, cut into bite-size pieces (2 cups)

2 medium oranges, peeled and sectioned

1 cup jicama cut into thin bite-size strips

1 medium red sweet pepper, cut into rings

lemony asparagus &
new potatoes with chicken

One brief stop to the produce aisle and another to the deli for chicken hot and fragrant from the rotisserie yield a meal that has overtures of springtime. Lemon peel and thyme add the grace notes.

1 pound whole tiny new potatoes, quartered

12 ounces asparagus spears, cut into 2-inch pieces

2 cups shredded or chopped deli-roasted chicken (10 ounces)

1 tablespoon olive oil or cooking oil

2 teaspoons snipped fresh thyme

1 teaspoon finely shredded lemon peel

¼ teaspoon salt

Start to finish: 25 minutes   Makes 4 servings

In a medium saucepan cook potatoes, covered, in a small amount of boiling water for 12 minutes. Add asparagus. Cook, covered, for 2 to 4 minutes more or until potatoes are tender and asparagus is crisp-tender. Drain vegetables; return to saucepan. Add chicken to saucepan.

Meanwhile, for dressing, in a small bowl whisk together the oil, thyme, lemon peel, and salt. Drizzle dressing over chicken mixture; toss lightly to coat.

Nutrition facts per serving: 319 cal., 13 g total fat (3 g sat. fat), 76 mg chol., 199 mg sodium, 27 g carbo., 2 g fiber, 23 g pro. Daily values: 17% vit. A, 49% vit. C, 3% calcium, 24% iron

chicken & broccoli
with creamy dressing

The smell of bacon cooking is irresistible. Top a robust mixture of broccoli slaw, nuggets of red apple, and chopped chicken with bacon, and watch diners materialize, forks in hand.

Start to finish: 20 minutes   Makes 4 servings

For dressing, in a small bowl stir together light mayonnaise dressing and vinegar; set aside.

In a large bowl toss together the broccoli, chicken, and apples. Pour dressing over chicken mixture; toss lightly to coat. Sprinkle with bacon.

Nutrition facts per serving: 327 cal., 18 g total fat (4 g sat. fat), 70 mg chol., 360 mg sodium, 18 g carbo., 4 g fiber, 26 g pro. Daily values: 15% vit. A, 144% vit. C, 4% calcium, 12% iron

cooked **chicken,** your way

There are several fast ways to prepare cooked chicken for salads. The easiest is to cover boneless or bone-in chicken breasts with water or stock and simmer on a stovetop until cooked through. Boneless breasts also can be broiled in the oven for about 6 minutes per side. If preparing large quantities, consider baking bone-in chicken breasts on a rack, skin side up, in a 350° oven for about 45 to 50 minutes. Use the meat for salads and save the juices, skin, bones, and trimmings to make stock for soup.

½   cup light mayonnaise dressing or salad dressing

2   tablespoons cider vinegar

4   cups broccoli flowerets or packaged shredded broccoli (broccoli slaw mix)

2   cups chopped cooked chicken (10 ounces)

2   small red apples, chopped

2   slices bacon, crisp-cooked, drained, and crumbled, or 2 tablespoons cooked bacon pieces

43

warm sweet potato, apple, & sausage salad

This main dish conjures up crisp autumn days and a fall bounty of sweet potatoes and apples. Leafy raw spinach provides a nutrient-rich base for a hearty salad that includes spicy turkey sausage.

44

- 1 pound sweet potatoes or yams, peeled and cut into ½-inch pieces (3 cups)
- 1 small onion, cut into thin wedges
- 2 tablespoons margarine or butter
- 1 pound cooked smoked turkey sausage, cut diagonally into ½-inch-thick slices
- 2 medium cooking apples, cut into wedges
- ½ cup bottled sweet-and-sour sauce
- ½ teaspoon caraway seed
- 6 cups torn fresh spinach

Start to finish: 30 minutes   Makes 4 servings

In a large skillet cook sweet potatoes and onion in margarine over medium heat about 10 minutes or until tender, stirring occasionally.

Stir in sausage, apples, sweet-and-sour sauce, and caraway seed. Cook, covered, over medium heat about 3 minutes or until apples are tender and sausage is heated through, stirring occasionally. (If mixture seems thick, add water, 1 tablespoon at a time, to make desired consistency.)

Place spinach on a large serving platter. Top with sweet potato mixture.

Nutrition facts per serving: 415 cal., 14 g total fat (3 g sat. fat), 72 mg chol., 196 mg sodium, 50 g carbo., 7 g fiber, 24 g pro. Daily values: 257% vit. A, 89% vit. C, 17% calcium, 31% iron

cabbage & chicken
with sesame dressing

Unchain yourself from slicing and dicing. Coleslaw mix provides the crunchy base for this Eastern-inspired meal, redolent of sesame oil, red pepper, and soy sauce.

¼ cup bottled Italian salad dressing

1 tablespoon soy sauce

1 teaspoon toasted sesame oil

⅛ to ¼ teaspoon crushed red pepper

3 cups packaged shredded cabbage with carrot (coleslaw mix)

2 cups chopped cooked chicken (10 ounces)

2 tablespoons snipped fresh cilantro

1 head Boston lettuce, separated into leaves

¼ cup slivered almonds, toasted

Start to finish: 20 minutes   Makes 4 servings

For dressing, in a small bowl combine salad dressing, soy sauce, sesame oil, and crushed red pepper. Set aside.

In a bowl toss together cabbage, chicken, and cilantro. Drizzle with dressing; toss lightly to coat.

Line 4 plates with lettuce leaves. Divide chicken mixture among plates. Sprinkle with almonds.

Nutrition facts per serving: 298 cal., 18 g total fat (3 g sat. fat), 68 mg chol., 457 mg sodium, 9 g carbo., 3 g fiber, 25 g pro. Daily values: 45% vit. A, 52% vit. C, 6% calcium, 12% iron

sesame oil: a little goes a long way

Toasted sesame oil is a flavoring oil, not a cooking oil, and is used sparingly in recipes because of its strong flavor. (There also is a lighter sesame oil that has very little sesame flavor.) Often, the toasted sesame oil is drizzled on a finished stir-fry dish for a crowning touch. Once opened, it should be kept in the refrigerator to prevent it from becoming rancid, and can be stored for up to a year.

broiled turkey salad with pineapple wedges

Want to intensify the sweet goodness of pineapple? Let it sizzle under a broiler and enjoy its caramelized flavor. Add warm strips of turkey and refreshing jicama for an arresting lineup that goes beyond the usual suspects.

Start to finish: 25 minutes   Makes 4 servings

Rinse turkey; pat dry. Spray the unheated rack of a broiler pan with non-stick coating. Arrange turkey and pineapple wedges on rack. Broil 4 to 5 inches from heat for 8 to 10 minutes or until turkey is tender and no longer pink. Turn pineapple once during broiling time. Cool; cut turkey into bite-size strips.

Divide lettuce among 4 plates. Arrange turkey, pineapple, jicama, and carrots atop lettuce.

For dressing, stir together yogurt, pineapple juice, curry powder, and pepper. Drizzle dressing over salads.

Nutritional facts per serving: 221 cal., 4 g total fat (1 g sat. fat), 61 mg chol., 95 mg sodium, 21 g carbo., 2 g fiber, 25 g pro. Daily values: 80% vit. A, 31% vit. C, 8% calcium, 12% iron

- 1 pound turkey breast tenderloin steaks
- Nonstick spray coating
- 12 fresh pineapple wedges
- 6 cups shredded lettuce
- 1 cup jicama cut into thin bite-size pieces
- 1 cup coarsely shredded carrots
- 1 6-ounce carton tropical- or pineapple-flavored fat-free yogurt
- 2 tablespoons pineapple juice or orange juice
- ½ teaspoon curry powder
- Dash pepper

savvy
seafood

asian grilled salmon salad

Fennel, one of the oldest cultivated plants, is used whole to spice sausages, crushed for tomato sauces, and often is added to poaching liquids for fish. Here, it is pressed into salmon steaks before grilling, making a toothsome base for dressed vegetables.

Start to finish: 25 minutes   Makes 4 servings

Snap off and discard woody bases from asparagus. Rinse fish; pat dry.

Brush asparagus spears and both sides of salmon lightly with oil. Press fennel seed onto both sides of salmon.

Place salmon on the greased rack of an uncovered grill directly over medium coals. Place asparagus on a piece of heavy foil on grill rack next to salmon. Grill for 8 to 12 minutes or until asparagus is tender and the fish begins to flake easily, turning once halfway through.

Meanwhile, line 4 plates with lettuce leaves. Place salmon atop greens. Arrange asparagus, tomato wedges, and enoki mushrooms around salmon. Drizzle with Asian Dressing.

Asian Dressing: In a screw-top jar combine 1 tablespoon salad oil, 1 tablespoon rice vinegar, 1 tablespoon soy sauce, 1 teaspoon toasted sesame oil, ¼ teaspoon sugar, and ¼ teaspoon grated gingerroot or ½ teaspoon chopped pickled ginger. Cover and shake well.

Nutrition facts per serving: 255 cal., 13 g total fat (2 g sat. fat), 31 mg chol., 368 mg sodium, 7 g carbo., 2 g fiber, 28 g pro. Daily values: 14% vit. A, 45% vit. C, 4% calcium, 15% iron

1   **pound asparagus spears**

4   **6- to 8-ounce salmon fillets or steaks, cut 1 inch thick**

1   **tablespoon garlic-flavored oil or olive oil**

1   **teaspoon fennel seed, crushed**

1   **head Bibb lettuce, separated into leaves**

1   **medium tomato, cut into thin wedges**

1   **cup enoki mushrooms (2 ounces)**

1   **recipe Asian Dressing**

wilted **sorrel** salad

There's no better way to serve dark, leafy greens than with a quick splash of hot bacon and onion dressing. The unexpected twist is the addition of quickly cooked fish fillets.

1 **pound fish fillets, such as orange roughy, sea bass, or salmon**

Lemon-pepper seasoning

4 **slices bacon**

1 **small red onion, sliced and separated into rings**

2 **tablespoons dry sherry**

2 **tablespoons honey**

8 **cups torn sorrel and/or fresh spinach**

Start to finish: 25 minutes Makes 4 servings

Rinse fish; pat dry. Arrange fish in a 2-quart square microwave-safe baking dish; tuck under thin edges. Sprinkle fish with lemon-pepper seasoning. Microwave on high until fish is opaque and flakes easily with a fork. (Allow 3 to 5 minutes for $\frac{1}{2}$-inch-thick fillets and 5 to 7 minutes for $\frac{3}{4}$-inch-thick fillets.)

Meanwhile, in a large skillet cook bacon over medium heat until crisp. Drain bacon, reserving 2 tablespoons drippings in skillet. Crumble bacon and set aside. Add onion to the reserved drippings in skillet. Cook and stir over medium heat until onion is tender. Stir in sherry and honey. Bring to boiling; remove from heat.

In a large bowl toss together sorrel and bacon. Pour sherry mixture over sorrel mixture; toss lightly to coat. Divide sorrel mixture among 4 plates. Top with fish.

Nutrition facts per serving: 211 cal., 5 g total fat (1 g sat. fat), 66 mg cholesterol, 317 mg sodium, 14 g carbo., 3 g fiber, 27 g pro. Daily values: 76% vit. A, 56% vit. C, 10% calcium, 23% iron

garden greens
with swordfish

Firm-fleshed fish, such as swordfish or tuna, slices well after cooking, the better to arrange atop arugula and other greens. They all are complemented by an assertive salad dressing made with roasted sweet peppers, conveniently available in a jar.

Start to finish: 30 minutes   Makes 4 servings

Rinse fish; pat dry. Brush fish with lemon juice. Stir together the Italian seasoning, garlic salt, and pepper; rub over fish. Place fish on the greased, unheated rack of a broiler pan.

Broil 4 inches from heat for 5 minutes. Using a wide spatula, carefully turn fish over. Broil 3 to 7 minutes more or until fish flakes easily with a fork. Cool; cut fish into thin bite-size strips.

Divide salad greens among 4 plates. Top with fish and tomatoes. Drizzle dressing over salads.

Roasted Pepper Dressing: In a blender container or food processor bowl, combine ½ of a 7-ounce jar roasted red sweet peppers, drained (½ cup); ¼ cup salad oil; 3 tablespoons vinegar; ¼ teaspoon salt; and dash ground red pepper. Cover and blend or process until nearly smooth. Cover and chill for up to 24 hours.

Nutrition facts per serving: 282 cal., 18 g total fat (3 g sat. fat), 45 mg chol., 374 mg sodium, 6 g carbo., 2 g fiber, 24 g pro. Daily values: 17% vit. A, 104% vit. C, 2% calcium, 13% iron

1 **pound swordfish or tuna steaks, cut 1 inch thick**

1 **tablespoon lemon juice**

1 **teaspoon dried Italian seasoning, crushed**

¼ **teaspoon garlic salt**

⅛ **teaspoon pepper**

6 **cups torn mixed salad greens**

12 **red and/or yellow baby pear tomatoes or cherry tomatoes, halved**

1 **recipe Roasted Pepper Dressing**

scandinavian shrimp salad

Create a Scandinavian smorgasbord all on one plate with vinaigrette-coated shrimp flanked by rye bread topped with cream cheese and cucumbers. A critical ingredient is dillweed, which is sprinkled atop the bread and snipped into the vinaigrette.

12 slices party rye bread or 12 large crackers

3 tablespoons reduced-fat cream cheese (Neufchâtel)

⅓ cup shredded cucumber

⅓ cup thinly sliced red onion

Fresh dill (optional)

6 cups torn mixed salad greens

12 ounces peeled, deveined, cooked shrimp

¼ cup bottled nonfat white wine vinaigrette salad dressing

1 tablespoon snipped fresh dill

Start to finish: 25 minutes   Makes 4 servings

Spread bread slices with cream cheese; top with cucumber and onion. If desired, sprinkle with dill.

Divide salad greens among 4 plates; top with shrimp. Stir together salad dressing and the 1 tablespoon dill; drizzle over salads. Serve with rye bread slices.

Nutrition facts per serving: 218 cal., 5 g total fat (2 g sat. fat), 174 mg chol., 641 mg sodium, 20 g carbo., 1 g fiber, 23 g pro. Daily values: 12% vit. A, 10% vit. C, 6% calcium, 26% iron

tossed salad with
shrimp & oranges

Sautéing shrimp is faster than fast food and a healthful change of pace, particularly when draped over fresh spinach leaves. Serve the shrimp with homemade croutons made from leftover sourdough bread.

54

2 oranges

  Orange juice

12 ounces peeled, deveined shrimp

1 teaspoon snipped fresh rosemary

2 tablespoons white wine vinegar

2 tablespoons salad oil

6 cups torn fresh spinach or torn mixed salad greens

1 small red onion, thinly sliced and separated into rings

Start to finish: 30 minutes   Makes 4 servings

Finely shred 1 teaspoon orange peel; set orange peel aside. Peel and section oranges over a bowl to catch juices; set orange sections aside. Measure juices and add additional orange juice to equal $\frac{1}{3}$ cup; set orange juice aside.

Rinse shrimp; pat dry. Cook shrimp in boiling, salted water for 1 to 3 minutes or until shrimp turn opaque; drain. Rinse with cold water; drain again. Set shrimp aside.

For dressing, in a small saucepan bring the reserved orange juice and the rosemary to boiling. Remove from heat; stir in the reserved orange peel, vinegar, and salad oil.

In a large bowl toss together spinach, onion rings, orange sections, and shrimp. Pour dressing over salad. Toss lightly to coat.

Nutrition facts per serving: 174 cal., 8 g total fat (1 g sat. fat), 131 mg chol., 216 mg sodium, 10 g carbo., 3 g fiber, 17 g pro. Daily values: 62% vit. A, 88% vit. C, 10% calcium, 30% iron

shrimp with chipotle vinaigrette

Play beat the clock with sautéed shrimp. Cooking time is less than five minutes, then you can leisurely fiddle with the spicy dressing and serve the shrimp as a warm counterpoint to chilled greens.

Start to finish: 30 minutes   Makes 4 servings

In a large skillet cook and stir shrimp in hot oil for 3 to 4 minutes or until shrimp turn opaque. Remove from heat; squeeze lime juice over shrimp. Set shrimp aside for up to 30 minutes to cool slightly.

Meanwhile, for vinaigrette, in a small mixing bowl whisk together the chipotle pepper, tomato juice, salad oil, sugar, and garlic.

To serve, divide salad greens among 4 plates. Top with shrimp and onion. Drizzle with vinaigrette.

Nutrition facts per serving: 159 cal., 8 g total fat (1 g sat. fat), 131 mg chol., 253 mg sodium, 6 g carbo., 3 g fiber, 16 g pro. Daily values: 38% vit. A, 54% vit. C, 6% calcium, 23% iron

12	ounces peeled, deveined medium shrimp
1	tablespoon cooking oil
1	tablespoon lime juice
½	to 1 teaspoon crushed dried chipotle pepper
⅓	cup tomato juice
1	tablespoon salad oil
¼	teaspoon sugar
1	clove garlic, minced
8	cups torn mixed salad greens, romaine, or spinach
½	cup sliced red onion

the **buzz** on **chipotle** peppers

Take ripe red jalapeño peppers, smoke them over wood, dry them, and you have chipotle (chih-POHT-lay) peppers. They are hot, but not as hot as cayenne or crushed red pepper. Crushed chipotle pepper has the same smoky, hot flavor and is sold bottled for convenience. If you can't find bottled crushed chipotle pepper, crush 1 to 2 small whole dried chipotle peppers with a mortar and pestle to get ½ to 1 teaspoon.

seared scallop
& spinach salad

Give an old favorite a new lease on life by adding sea scallops to the usual lineup in a bacon-spinach salad. The scallops are dusted with chili powder and red pepper before searing—a guaranteed wake-up call for eaters.

Start to finish: 30 minutes   Makes 4 servings

Rinse scallops; pat dry. Set scallops aside. In a large bowl toss together spinach, mushrooms, and carrots; set aside.

In a large nonstick skillet cook bacon over medium heat until crisp. Drain bacon, reserving 1 tablespoon drippings in skillet.

In a medium bowl combine chili powder and ground red pepper; add scallops, tossing lightly to coat.

Cook scallops in reserved bacon drippings over medium heat for 1 to 3 minutes or until scallops turn opaque. Remove scallops from skillet; set aside. Add chutney, water, and mustard to skillet. Cook over medium-high heat until hot and bubbly; spoon over spinach mixture, tossing lightly to coat.

Divide spinach mixture among 4 plates. Top with scallops. Sprinkle with bacon.

Nutrition facts per serving: 160 cal., 4 g total fat (1 g sat. fat), 22 mg chol., 324 mg sodium, 19 g carbo., 5 g fiber, 14 g pro. Daily values: 154% vit. A, 63% vit. C, 13% calcium, 32% iron

½ **pound sea scallops**

8 **cups torn fresh spinach**

2 **cups sliced fresh mushrooms**

1 **cup shredded carrots**

4 **slices bacon, cut into ½-inch pieces**

½ **teaspoon chili powder**

⅛ **to ¼ teaspoon ground red pepper**

¼ **to ⅓ cup chutney, snipped**

¼ **cup water**

1 **to 2 teaspoons Dijon-style mustard**

scallop stir-fry salad

Spinach and cabbage get a coating of many colors with a sauce containing baby corn, orange juice, and sweet bay scallops. It's a cure for the common meal.

2 tablespoons orange juice

2 tablespoons reduced-sodium soy sauce

1 tablespoon rice wine vinegar or white wine vinegar

1 teaspoon sugar

1 teaspoon toasted sesame oil

12 ounces bay scallops

1 cup fresh snow pea pods, strings and tips removed

2 tablespoons cooking oil

1 medium red sweet pepper, coarsely chopped

½ cup sliced green onions

1 8-ounce jar baby corn, rinsed and drained

2 cups shredded Chinese cabbage

2 cups shredded fresh spinach or romaine

Start to finish: 30 minutes   Makes 4 servings

Stir together orange juice, soy sauce, vinegar, sugar, and sesame oil; set aside. Rinse scallops; pat dry. Halve pea pods lengthwise. Pour 1 tablespoon oil into a wok or large skillet. Preheat over medium-high heat. Stir-fry scallops in hot oil for 3 to 4 minutes or until scallops are opaque.

Remove scallops from wok. Add remaining oil to wok. Stir-fry pea pods, sweet pepper, and green onions for 2 to 3 minutes or until crisp-tender. Add scallops, corn, and orange juice mixture to wok. Cook and stir about 1 minute or until heated through.

In a large bowl combine cabbage and spinach. Top with scallop mixture. Toss lightly to combine.

Nutrition facts per serving: 171 cal., 9 g total fat (1g sat. fat), 26 mg chol., 421 mg sodium, 10 g carbo., 3 g fiber, 15 g pro. Daily values: 40% vit. A, 113% vit. C, 10% calcium, 21% iron

scallop selection 101

The smallest scallops on the market are the light pink or tan bay scallops, sometimes known as cape scallops. The larger, white scallops are sea scallops. If only sea scallops are available, you may want to cut them in half before cooking, slicing against the grain.

curried **crab** salad

Dispel the myth: Not all curries are hot. Packaged curry powder purchased at a grocery store is generally a sweet mixture of as many as 20 spices. It does magical things when mixed in a sauce and added to crabmeat.

Start to finish: 20 minutes   Makes 3 servings

In a large bowl combine fresh fruit, crabmeat, and celery; set aside.

For dressing, stir together light mayonnaise dressing, yogurt, milk, and curry powder.

Divide salad greens among 3 plates. Top with crab mixture and drizzle with dressing. If desired, sprinkle with raspberries.

Nutrition facts per serving: 200 cal., 9 g total fat (2 g sat. fat), 58 mg chol., 361 mg sodium, 17 g carbo., 2 g fiber, 14 g pro. Daily values: 21% vit. A, 62% vit. C, 11% calcium, 9% iron

- **2 cups cut-up fresh fruit (such as pineapple, cantaloupe, honeydew melon, or strawberries)**
- **1 6-ounce package frozen crabmeat, thawed**
- **¾ cup sliced celery**
- **¼ cup light mayonnaise dressing or salad dressing**
- **¼ cup plain low-fat yogurt**
- **2 tablespoons skim milk**
- **½ teaspoon curry powder**
- **4 cups torn mixed salad greens**
- **Fresh raspberries (optional)**

going with
the grain

grilled vegetable salad with garlic dressing

Vegetables, sweet and smoky from the grill, give pasta and cheese a jolt of flavor and color. By doing the grilling ahead, and storing the savory dressing in the refrigerator, this maximum-impact dish is done in the time it takes to simmer pasta.

Start to finish: 25 minutes   Makes 4 servings

Halve sweet peppers lengthwise; remove and discard stems, seeds, and membranes. Brush sweet peppers, eggplants, and zucchini with oil. To grill, place vegetables on the grill rack directly over medium-hot coals. Grill, uncovered, for 8 to 12 minutes or until vegetables are tender, turning occasionally. Remove vegetables from grill; cool slightly. Cut vegetables into 1-inch pieces.

Meanwhile, cook pasta according to package directions; drain. Rinse with cold water; drain again. In a large bowl combine pasta and grilled vegetables. Pour dressing over salad. Toss lightly to coat. Stir in cheese; sprinkle with parsley.

Roasted Garlic Dressing: In a screw-top jar combine 3 tablespoons balsamic vinegar or red wine vinegar, 2 tablespoons olive oil, 1 tablespoon water, 1 teaspoon bottled roasted minced garlic, ¼ teaspoon salt, and ¼ teaspoon pepper. Cover and shake well.

Nutrition facts per serving: 369 cal., 19 g total fat (6 g sat. fat), 61 mg chol., 317 mg sodium, 40 g carbo., 5 g fiber, 12 g pro. Daily values: 38% vit. A, 113% vit. C, 12% calcium, 18% iron

Note: If using sunburst or pattypan squash, precook for 3 minutes in a small amount of boiling water before grilling.

- 2 red and/or yellow sweet peppers
- 2 Japanese eggplants, halved lengthwise
- 2 medium zucchini or yellow summer squash, halved lengthwise, or 8 to 10 yellow sunburst or pattypan squash*
- 1 tablespoon olive oil
- 2 cups dried tortiglioni or rigatoni
- 1 recipe Roasted Garlic Dressing
- ¾ cup cubed fontina cheese (3 ounces)
- 1 to 2 tablespoons snipped fresh Italian parsley or parsley

mediterranean
couscous salad

This Mediterranean meal is fast, flavorful, and healthy. A lemon and oregano dressing enlivens feta cheese and vegetables on a bed of quick-cooking couscous.

1¾ cups water

1 cup quick-cooking couscous

1 recipe Lemon-Oregano Vinaigrette

1 medium red sweet pepper,
 chopped

½ cup chopped, seeded cucumber

¼ cup sliced or chopped pitted
 Greek black olives or ripe olives

¼ cup crumbled feta cheese

1 recipe Pita Chips or crisp crackers

Start to finish: 25 minutes   Makes 4 servings

In a small saucepan bring water to boiling. Remove from heat; stir in the couscous. Let stand, covered, for 5 minutes; fluff with fork.

Place couscous in large bowl. Drizzle vinaigrette over couscous. Cool for 10 minutes. Add sweet pepper, cucumber, and olives; toss to combine. Sprinkle with cheese. Serve with Pita Chips.

Lemon-Oregano Vinaigrette: In a screw-top jar combine 3 tablespoons lemon juice; 2 tablespoons olive oil; 1 tablespoon snipped fresh mint or ¼ teaspoon dried mint, crushed; and 1 tablespoon snipped fresh oregano or ¾ teaspoon dried oregano, crushed. Cover and shake well.

Pita Chips: Cut 2 pita bread rounds in half horizontally; cut each half into 6 wedges. Arrange wedges in a single layer on a baking sheet. Brush lightly with 1 tablespoon olive oil or spray with nonstick spray coating. Sprinkle with ¼ to ½ teaspoon garlic salt. Bake in a 400° oven for 6 to 8 minutes or until crisp and lightly browned.

Nutrition facts per serving: 392 cal., 14 g total fat (3 g sat. fat), 6 mg chol., 287 mg sodium, 57 g carbo., 8 g fiber, 10 g pro. Daily values: 24% vit. A, 70% vit. C, 10% calcium, 19% iron

gazpacho pasta salad

The flavors of a famed Spanish soup, gazpacho—a cold soup featuring tomatoes, garlic, vinegar, and cucumber—meet Italian cheese tortellini, and the marriage is a huge success. Crunchy croutons complete the combination.

Start to finish: 25 minutes   Makes 4 servings

Cook pasta according to package directions; drain. Rinse with cold water; drain again.

In a large bowl combine pasta, tomatoes, cucumber, and capers.

For dressing, in a screw-top jar combine oil, vinegar, mustard, and garlic. Cover and shake well. Pour dressing over salad. Toss lightly to coat.

Line 4 plates with lettuce leaves. Divide salad among lettuce-lined plates. Sprinkle with croutons.

Nutrition facts per serving: 352 cal., 16 g total fat (3 g sat. fat), 30 mg chol., 375 mg sodium, 43 g carbo., 2 g fiber, 12 g pro. Daily values: 9% vit. A, 39% vit. C, 11% calcium, 16% iron

1 9-ounce package refrigerated cheese tortellini

2 cups cherry tomatoes, halved

1 cup chopped cucumber

2 tablespoons capers, drained

3 tablespoons olive oil

3 tablespoons white wine vinegar

2 teaspoons honey mustard

1 clove garlic, minced

4 leaf lettuce leaves

1 cup croutons

foreign intrigue: **the caper caper**

They're an integral ingredient in tartar sauce, a good foil to cream sauces, and a traditional accompaniment to sliced salmon. What are they? Green capers are unopened flower buds on a bush that's grown primarily in Europe. The buds are packed in a vinegar brine and usually are drained, and sometimes rinsed, before using. Tangy and pungent, they have a flavor that can't easily be substituted.

caribbean **pasta** salad

Tangy blue cheese provides a snappy comeback to ripe tropical fruits in this refreshing entrée. Lean ham or turkey strips make it a full-fledged meal.

8 ounces dried bow-tie pasta

1 papaya or mango, seeded, peeled, and cut into bite-size chunks (1½ cups)

1 cup pineapple chunks

4 ounces lean cooked ham or cooked smoked turkey, cut into bite-size strips (about ¾ cup)

½ cup chopped red sweet pepper

½ cup sliced green onions

½ cup bottled blue cheese salad dressing

2 tablespoons snipped fresh cilantro

Start to finish: 25 minutes   Makes 4 servings

Cook pasta according to package directions; drain. Rinse with cold water; drain again.

In a large bowl combine pasta, papaya, pineapple, ham, sweet pepper, and green onions. Pour salad dressing over salad. Toss lightly to coat. Sprinkle with cilantro.

Nutrition facts per serving: 438 cal., 20 g total fat (4 g sat. fat), 82 mg chol., 688 mg sodium, 51 g carbo., 2 g fiber, 15 g pro. Daily values: 32% vit. A, 121% vit. C, 5% calcium, 21% iron

tropical timesavers

One of the happy innovations in the supermarket today is jars of chilled sliced papaya and mango, available year-round. Conveniently peeled and always at the peak of ripeness, they are custom-made for salad meals. In season, sliced nectarines can be called upon.

prosciutto & melon salad

One of the classic appetizers of all time is the partnership of prosciutto and melon. Expand its horizons with the addition of shredded and chopped vegetables, and appealing ribbed pasta shaped like tiny radiators, called radiatore.

Start to finish: 25 minutes   Makes 4 servings

Cook pasta according to package directions; drain. Rinse with cold water; drain again.

In a large bowl combine pasta, tomatoes, yellow summer squash, peas, prosciutto, and basil. Pour salad dressing over salad. Toss lightly to coat.

To serve, fan 3 slices of cantaloupe on each of 4 plates; top with salad.

Nutrition facts per serving: 252 cal., 5 g total fat (0 g sat. fat), 0 mg chol., 308 mg sodium, 43 g carbo., 3 g fiber, 11 g pro. Daily values: 26% vit. A, 90% vit. C, 2% calcium, 16% iron

2	cups dried radiatore
1½	cups coarsely chopped tomatoes (2 medium)
1	cup shredded yellow summer squash or zucchini (1 medium)
½	cup frozen peas
2	ounces prosciutto or cooked ham, chopped (about ⅓ cup)
¼	cup snipped fresh basil
⅓	cup bottled balsamic vinaigrette salad dressing
12	thin slices cantaloupe

mexican fiesta salad

Prepare this creamy chilled salad in the morning and look forward all day to a hearty, corn-and-bean-studded treat. Lime and cilantro infuse the sour cream dressing.

- 2 cups dried penne or rotini
- ½ cup frozen whole kernel corn
- ½ cup light dairy sour cream
- ⅓ cup mild or medium chunky salsa
- 1 tablespoon snipped fresh cilantro
- 1 tablespoon lime juice
- 1 15-ounce can black beans, rinsed and drained
- 3 medium plum tomatoes, chopped (1 cup)
- 1 medium zucchini, chopped (1 cup)
- ½ cup shredded sharp cheddar cheese (2 ounces)

Start to finish: 30 minutes   Makes 4 servings

Cook pasta according to package directions, adding the corn the last 5 minutes of cooking. Drain pasta and corn. Rinse with cold water; drain again.

Meanwhile, for dressing, in a small mixing bowl stir together sour cream, salsa, cilantro, and lime juice. Set dressing aside.

In a large bowl combine pasta mixture, black beans, tomatoes, zucchini, and cheese. Pour dressing over pasta mixture. Toss lightly to coat. Serve immediately or, if desired, cover and chill for up to 24 hours. (After chilling, if necessary, stir in enough milk to make desired consistency.)

Nutrition facts per serving: 373 cal., 9 g total fat (4 g sat. fat), 19 mg chol., 470 mg sodium, 61 g carbo., 7 g fiber, 20 g pro. Daily values: 15% vit. A, 36% vit. C, 15% calcium, 23% iron

white beans with tuna

Canned beans eliminate soaking and cooking chores, and this recipe works well with any variety on hand. The tuna and dressing come from the pantry as well, making this a good spur-of-the-moment choice.

1 15-ounce can white kidney beans, black beans, or red kidney beans, rinsed and drained

1 cup thinly sliced celery

⅓ to ½ cup desired bottled creamy salad dressing, such as ranch, garlic, Parmesan, honey Dijon, or Italian

¼ cup finely chopped red onion

1 6½-ounce can chunk white tuna (water pack), drained and broken into chunks

1 head Boston or Bibb lettuce, separated into leaves

2 medium red sweet peppers

2 tablespoons snipped fresh dill

Start to finish: 20 minutes   Makes 4 servings

In a medium bowl stir together beans, celery, salad dressing, and onion. Gently stir in tuna. If desired, cover and chill for up to 24 hours.

To serve, line 4 plates with lettuce. Halve sweet peppers lengthwise; remove and discard stems, seeds, and membranes. Cut each pepper half lengthwise into 3 strips. Divide pepper strips among lettuce-lined plates. Spoon bean mixture over pepper strips. Sprinkle with dill.

Nutrition facts per serving: 203 cal., 9 g total fat (1 g sat. fat), 13 mg chol., 349 mg sodium, 20 g carbo., 6 g fiber, 19 g pro. Daily values: 45% vit. A, 122% vit. C, 4% calcium, 13% iron

texas caviar salad

This popular appetizer becomes an entrée with the addition of tomato wedges. Black-eyed peas provide protein, and crushed cumin seeds and jalapeño peppers give the mixture its Lone Star kick.

Start to finish: 25 minutes   Makes 4 servings

In a medium skillet cook yellow summer squash, jalapeño peppers, cumin seed, and garlic in hot oil about 8 minutes or until the squash is tender, stirring occasionally. Remove from heat; cool slightly.

In a large bowl toss together squash mixture, black-eyed peas, green onions, vinegar, and cilantro. If desired, cover and chill up to 24 hours.

Before serving, toss tomato wedges into salad.

Nutrition facts per serving: 265 cal., 9 g total fat (1 g sat. fat), 0 mg chol., 521 mg sodium, 38 g carbo., 11 g fiber, 12 g pro. Daily values: 6% vit. A, 36% vit. C, 6% calcium, 8% iron

- 2 cups thinly sliced yellow summer squash
- 1 to 2 jalapeño peppers, seeded and chopped (about 2 tablespoons)
- ½ teaspoon cumin seed, crushed
- 2 cloves garlic, minced
- 2 tablespoons cooking oil
- 2 16-ounce cans black-eyed peas, rinsed and drained
- 2 green onions, sliced
- 2 tablespoons vinegar
- 2 teaspoons snipped fresh cilantro
- 3 medium tomatoes, cut into thin wedges

peppers: choose **your** weapon

Peppers carry heat ratings, expressed in Scoville units, to serve as a guide when deciding how fiery a dish will be. Habanero and pequín chilies are at the top of the chart; ancho and poblano chilies are at the mild end. Jalapeños and Anaheim or New Mexican chilies are roughly in the middle. All hot peppers contain oils that can burn eyes, lips, and sensitive skin, so wear plastic gloves while preparing them, and wash your hands and under fingernails thoroughly afterward.

italian mozzarella salad

Fresh mozzarella is a softer, more delicately flavored cousin of the cheese slathered on pizza. Celebrate its incomparable flavor atop a salad of mixed beans, given spark by a garlicky basil dressing. (Pictured on the cover.)

1 15-ounce can black beans or garbanzo beans, rinsed and drained

1 15-ounce can butter beans or great northern beans, rinsed and drained

1 small cucumber, quartered lengthwise and sliced (1 cup)

2 red and/or yellow tomatoes, cut into thin wedges

¼ cup thinly sliced green onions

Basil Dressing or ½ cup bottled oil and vinegar salad dressing

8 ounces round- or log-shaped fresh mozzarella or part-skim scamorze

Start to finish: 20 minutes   Makes 4 servings

In a large bowl combine beans, cucumber, tomatoes, and green onions. Add dressing; toss lightly to coat. Cut cheese into thin slices; gently toss with bean mixture.

Basil Dressing: In a screw-top jar combine ¼ cup red wine vinegar; ¼ cup olive oil or salad oil; 1 tablespoon snipped fresh basil or 1 teaspoon dried basil, crushed; 1 teaspoon Dijon-style mustard; ¼ teaspoon crushed red pepper; and 1 clove garlic, minced. Cover and shake well. Makes about ½ cup. If desired, chill up to 2 days.

Nutrition facts per serving: 434 cal., 23 g total fat (8 g sat. fat), 32 mg chol., 919 mg sodium, 37 g carbo., 6 g fiber, 27 g pro. Daily values: 16% vit. A, 24% vit. C, 36% calcium, 24% iron

the allure of **fresh mozzarella**

It's worth seeking out Italian markets, good cheese shops, and well-stocked gourmet delis to find fresh mozzarella. It is much softer, moister, and more elastic than the solid mozzarella that's a staple on pizza. In Italy, it's often served sliced in tomato salads or with fresh fruit for dessert. A similar Italian cheese is scamorze (also spelled scamorza or scamorzo) that's often aged and smoked, but eaten fresh when young, like mozzarella.

autumn vegetable salad with hot bacon dressing

Fresh, barely cooked Brussels sprouts are astonishingly good, a different creature altogether from the steam-table variety. When mixed with garbanzo beans and carrots, and given the hot bacon dressing treatment, they'll be a regular at the table.

Start to finish: 30 minutes   Makes 4 servings

Trim stems and remove any wilted leaves from fresh Brussels sprouts; wash. Cut any large Brussels sprouts in half lengthwise. Cook, covered, in a small amount of boiling water for 2 minutes. Add carrots; cover and cook for 8 to 10 minutes more or until vegetables are crisp-tender. (Or, cook frozen sprouts according to package directions, adding carrots the last 8 to 10 minutes of cooking.)

Meanwhile, in a large skillet cook the bacon over medium heat until crisp. Drain bacon, reserving 2 tablespoons drippings in skillet. Crumble bacon and set aside.

Stir vinegar, sugar, and savory into drippings. Bring to boiling; add cooked vegetables and garbanzo beans. Cook and stir for 1 to 2 minutes or until heated through.

In a large bowl toss together romaine and vegetable mixture. Top with crumbled bacon.

Nutrition facts per serving: 275 cal., 12 g total fat (4 g sat. fat), 11 mg chol., 530 mg sodium, 36 g carbo., 12 g fiber, 11 g pro. Daily values: 164% vit. A, 153% vit. C, 11% calcium, 34% iron

2 cups Brussels sprouts or one 10-ounce package frozen Brussels sprouts

1½ cups packaged, peeled baby carrots, halved lengthwise

4 slices bacon

¼ cup wine vinegar

1 tablespoon sugar

1 tablespoon snipped fresh summer savory or basil or ½ teaspoon dried savory or basil, crushed

1 15-ounce can garbanzo beans, rinsed and drained

8 cups torn romaine or torn mixed salad greens

middle eastern
bulgur-spinach salad

Bulgur or cracked wheat is a Middle Eastern staple. It's often cooked with lamb, but this vegetarian mélange of grain, fruits, and vegetables is equally satisfying and boasts a preparation that's simplicity itself.

Start to finish: 30 minutes   Makes 4 servings

In a medium bowl combine bulgur and boiling water. Let stand about 10 minutes or until bulgur has absorbed all the water. Cool 15 minutes.

Meanwhile, for dressing, in a small mixing bowl stir together yogurt, vinaigrette salad dressing, parsley, and cumin.

In a large bowl combine bulgur, spinach, garbanzo beans, apple, onion, and, if desired, raisins. Pour dressing over salad. Toss lightly to coat.

Nutrition facts per serving: 340 cal., 11 g total fat (2 g sat. fat), 2 mg chol., 673 mg sodium, 53 g carbo., 16 g fiber, 13 g pro. Daily values: 58% vit. A, 55% vit. C, 16% calcium, 40% iron

- 1 cup bulgur
- 1 cup boiling water
- ½ cup plain yogurt
- ¼ cup bottled red wine vinaigrette salad dressing
- 2 tablespoons snipped fresh parsley
- ½ teaspoon ground cumin
- 6 cups torn fresh spinach
- 1 15-ounce can garbanzo beans, rinsed and drained
- 1 cup coarsely chopped apple
- ½ of a medium red onion, thinly sliced and separated into rings
- 3 tablespoons raisins (optional)

toasted barley **salad**

Rescue barley from its supporting role in vegetable soups and make it the headliner in this cold salad that's studded with butter beans and chopped fruit. By toasting it first, barley's rich, nutty flavor shines through.

1½ **cups quick-cooking barley**

2 **cups water**

1 **teaspoon instant chicken bouillon granules**

2 **tablespoons light mayonnaise dressing or salad dressing**

⅓ **cup plain fat-free yogurt**

2 **tablespoons lemon juice or orange juice**

¼ **teaspoon crushed red pepper**

¼ **teaspoon dry mustard**

1 **15-ounce can butter beans, rinsed and drained**

1 **cup chopped apple or one 11-ounce can mandarin orange sections, drained**

⅓ **cup sliced green onions**

Prep: 25 minutes   Chill: 30 minutes   Makes 5 servings

In a large skillet cook and stir barley over medium heat about 5 minutes or until toasted and golden brown. Remove from heat.

Carefully stir in water and bouillon granules. Bring to boiling. Reduce heat and simmer, covered, for 10 to 12 minutes or until barley is tender and most of the liquid is absorbed. Remove from heat. Spoon barley into a shallow baking pan and place in the freezer for about 30 minutes.*

For dressing, stir together light mayonnaise dressing, yogurt, lemon juice, crushed red pepper, and dry mustard. In a large bowl stir together barley, beans, apple, and green onions. Stir in dressing.

Nutrition facts per serving: 323 cal., 4 g total fat (0 g sat. fat), 0 mg chol., 302 mg sodium, 63 g carbo., 9 g fiber, 11 g pro. Daily values: 4% vit. A, 18% vit. C, 4% calcium, 15% iron

Note: If desired, cover and chill the barley for 2 to 24 hours in the refrigerator.

italian bread salad

Peasant fare—day-old bread, tomatoes, and onions—becomes a substantial supper fit for any table with well-chosen additions of cheese, basil, and vinaigrette. It's a perfect solution to a bumper crop of sweet, vine-ripened tomatoes.

Start to finish: 25 minutes   Makes 4 servings

In a large bowl toss together bread, tomatoes, cheese, basil, and green onions. Drizzle vinaigrette over salad. Toss lightly to coat.

Red Wine Vinaigrette: In a screw-top jar combine ¼ cup olive oil; 2 tablespoons red wine vinegar or raspberry vinegar; 1 to 2 cloves garlic, minced; ¼ teaspoon salt; and ¼ teaspoon pepper. Cover and shake well.

Nutrition facts per serving: 383 cal., 22 g total fat (6 g sat. fat), 22 mg chol., 582 mg sodium, 35 g carbo., 1 g fiber, 12 g pro. Daily values: 14% vit. A, 37% vit. C, 17% calcium, 15% iron

5   cups torn bite-size pieces (or 1-inch cubes) day-old Italian or wheat bread

2   cups chopped tomatoes

1   cup cubed fresh mozzarella cheese (4 ounces)

¼   cup thinly sliced fresh basil

¼   cup thinly sliced green onions

Red Wine Vinaigrette or ½ cup bottled red wine vinaigrette salad dressing

peppered pork
& apricot salad

Dazzle guests with a main-dish salad whose vibrant colors—bright green, apricot, and black and cream—make a statement on a serving platter. Use quick-cooking pork tenderloin, then slice it into appealing medallions.

1 12-ounce pork tenderloin

1 teaspoon coarsely ground pepper

1 6-ounce package long-grain and wild rice mix

½ cup snipped dried apricots

¼ cup bottled nonfat Italian salad dressing

2 green onions, thinly sliced

2 tablespoons frozen orange juice concentrate, thawed

½ cup frozen peas

Fresh apricots, pitted and sliced (optional)

Start to finish: 50 minutes   Makes 4 servings

Place pork on a rack in a shallow roasting pan. Sprinkle the pepper evenly over pork. Roast in a 425° oven about 30 minutes or until a meat thermometer reaches 160°. Remove from oven; cover loosely with foil. Let stand for 10 minutes.

Meanwhile, prepare rice mix according to package directions, adding dried apricots the last 5 minutes of cooking. Spread in a shallow baking pan and cool for 20 minutes.

For dressing, in a small bowl combine salad dressing, green onions, and orange juice concentrate. In a large bowl combine rice mixture and peas; drizzle with dressing. Toss lightly to coat.

Spoon rice mixture onto a large serving platter. Cut tenderloin crosswise into thin slices; arrange slices over rice mixture. If desired, garnish with fresh apricots.

Nutrition facts per serving: 356 cal., 6 g total fat (2 g sat. fat), 61 mg chol., 1,056 mg sodium, 50 g carbo., 2 g fiber, 25 g pro. Daily values: 17% vit. A, 32% vit. C, 27% calcium, 4% iron

To make ahead: Cover and chill rice mixture and meat slices separately for up to 24 hours. Let stand at room temperature for no more than 30 minutes before serving.

brown rice & asparagus salad with shrimp

You've **run** out of excuses not to serve brown rice—it now comes in a quick-cooking variety that's ready in just 10 minutes. Its nutty flavor combines well with shrimp and asparagus, tempered with sweet-hot mustard and vivid bits of dried tomatoes.

8 ounces asparagus, trimmed and cut into 1½-inch pieces

3 cups cooked brown rice, chilled

8 ounces peeled, deveined, cooked shrimp

3 tablespoons chopped oil-packed dried tomatoes, drained

2 tablespoons sweet-hot mustard

¼ cup sliced almonds, toasted

Start to finish: 20 minutes   Makes 4 servings

Cook asparagus, covered, in a small amount of boiling water for 3 to 6 minutes or until crisp-tender. Drain; rinse under cold water.

In a large bowl toss together asparagus, rice, shrimp, and tomatoes. Add mustard; toss lightly to coat. Sprinkle with almonds.

Nutrition facts per serving: 296 cal., 7 g total fat (1 g sat. fat), 111 mg chol., 242 mg sodium, 39 g carbo., 4 g fiber, 18 g pro. Daily values: 7% vit. A, 28% vit. C, 6% calcium, 21% iron

fire-&-ice rice salad

Refreshing and bracing, this chilled salad plays both sweet and hot. Papaya and honey work with picante sauce and lime juice to bring a complex set of flavors to a canvas of white rice and shrimp.

Start to finish: 15 minutes   Makes 3 servings

In a medium bowl combine rice, papaya, and shrimp.

For dressing, in a small bowl combine picante sauce, honey, lime juice, and oil; mix well. Pour dressing over rice mixture; toss lightly to coat. If desired, cover and chill for up to 6 hours.

To serve, line 3 plates with lettuce. Top with salad. Sprinkle with cilantro.

Nutrition facts per serving: 348 cal., 4 g total fat (1 g sat. fat), 74 mg chol., 286 mg sodium, 64 g carbo., 1 g fiber, 13 g pro. Daily values: 15% vit. A, 70% vit. C, 4% calcium, 24% iron

2 cups cooked rice, chilled

1 cup chopped papaya or nectarines

4 ounces peeled, deveined, cooked
    shrimp, chilled

⅓ cup picante sauce

2 tablespoons honey

2 tablespoons lime juice

2 teaspoons olive oil or salad oil

    Lettuce leaves

2 teaspoons snipped fresh cilantro
    or parsley

potluck
picks

antipasto on a stick

Salami, vegetables, and cheesy tortellini are marinated overnight, making this a cinch to fix today for travel tomorrow. Serve slices of crusty bread to catch the drips as you eat your antipasto off of skewers (no serving utensils required).

Prep: 25 minutes   Chill: 2 to 24 hours   Makes 8 servings

Fold salami slices in quarters. On 16 short or 8 long wooden skewers, alternately thread salami, tortellini, artichoke halves, olives, pepperoncini, and tomatoes. Place kabobs in a plastic food storage container.

Stir together the ½ cup salad dressing and garlic; drizzle over kabobs. Cover and chill for 2 to 24 hours.

Brush bread slices with additional salad dressing. Place bread slices on the unheated rack of a broiler pan. Broil 4 to 5 inches from the heat for 1 minute or until slices are golden brown. Cool. Serve kabobs with toasted bread slices.

Nutrition facts per serving: 233 cal., 13 g total fat (4 g sat. fat), 31 mg chol., 1,020 mg sodium, 19 g carbo., 2 g fiber, 11 g pro. Daily values: 2% vit. A, 12% vit. C, 4% calcium, 10% iron

Note: If desired, substitute 1 cup (4 ounces) cubed provolone or mozzarella cheese for the tortellini.

½ pound thinly sliced salami or other desired meat

½ of a 9-ounce package refrigerated cheese-filled tortellini, cooked and drained (about 40)*

1 14-ounce can artichoke hearts, drained and halved

8 large pitted ripe olives

8 pepperoncini salad peppers

8 red or yellow cherry tomatoes

½ cup bottled reduced-calorie or nonfat Italian salad dressing

1 large clove garlic, minced

16 thin slices baguette-style French bread

Bottled reduced-calorie or nonfat Italian salad dressing

artichoke-dill
potato salad with chicken

Lift potato salad out of its ho-hum doldrums with marinated artichoke hearts, chopped dill pickle, and attention-getting lemon-pepper seasoning. Add cooked chicken, and it takes center stage on the menu.

82

- 3 pounds whole tiny new potatoes
- 1 cup light mayonnaise dressing or salad dressing
- ½ cup chopped onion
- 2 tablespoons chopped dill pickle
- 2 tablespoons wine vinegar
- 2 tablespoons Dijon-style mustard
- 1 tablespoon snipped fresh dill or 1½ teaspoons dried dillweed, crushed
- 1½ teaspoons lemon-pepper seasoning
- 2 cups chopped, cooked chicken (10 ounces)
- 2 6-ounce jars marinated artichoke hearts, drained and cut up
- 2 hard-cooked eggs, peeled and chopped

Prep: 30 minutes Chill: 4 to 24 hours Makes 10 to 12 servings

Cook potatoes, covered, in boiling, lightly salted water 20 minutes or just until tender. Drain. Cool potatoes; cut into bite-size pieces.

Meanwhile, in a very large bowl stir together light mayonnaise dressing, onion, dill pickle, vinegar, mustard, dill, and lemon-pepper seasoning. Gently fold in potatoes, chicken, artichoke hearts, and eggs. Cover and chill for 4 to 24 hours. Stir gently before serving.

Nutrition facts per serving: 320 cal., 14 g total fat (3 g sat. fat), 70 mg chol., 593 mg sodium, 36 g carbo., 2 g fiber, 14 g pro. Daily values: 4% vit. A, 42% vit. C, 3% calcium, 20% iron

take-along tips

Transporting salads long-distance isn't a problem when meats, fish, eggs, cheeses, and dairy products are kept thoroughly chilled. Tuck ice packs into an insulated container and begin your journey with a cold salad that has been refrigerated overnight. Serve the salad within 2 hours. For tender mixed green salads, pack the dressing separately and toss right before serving. Ditto for crisp garnishes such as nuts or croutons.

ginger-peanut pasta salad

This versatile recipe will work with nearly any fresh vegetable that's available and is successful with or without shrimp or chicken. The key elements that give the dish its character are the gingery dressing and the sprinkling of chopped peanuts.

Prep: 25 minutes   Chill: 2 to 8 hours   Makes 8 servings

Cook pasta according to package directions. If using the pea pods, add them the last 30 seconds of cooking. Drain pasta and pea pods. Rinse with cold water; drain again.

In a large bowl combine the pasta mixture, desired vegetables, shrimp, green onions, and, if desired, cilantro. Drizzle the dressing over pasta mixture; toss lightly to coat. Cover and chill for 2 to 8 hours.

Just before serving, toss salad and sprinkle with peanuts.

Ginger Salad Dressing: In a screw-top jar combine ¼ cup salad oil, 3 tablespoons rice vinegar, 2 tablespoons sugar, 2 tablespoons soy sauce, 1 teaspoon grated gingerroot, and ½ teaspoon chili oil or several dashes bottled hot pepper sauce. Cover and shake well. Chill dressing for up to 3 days. Shake dressing before using.

Nutrition facts per serving: 276 cal., 11 g total fat (2 g sat. fat), 69 mg chol., 395 mg sodium, 31 g carbo., 2 g fiber, 14 g pro. Daily values: 39% vit. A, 64% vit. C, 3% calcium, 19% iron

- 8 ounces dried rotini
- 4 cups mixed cut-up vegetables, such as snow pea pods, kohlrabi, cucumbers, carrots, red or green sweet peppers, and radishes
- 2 cups cooked shrimp or chopped cooked chicken (10 ounces)
- ½ cup sliced green onions
- 3 tablespoons snipped fresh cilantro (optional)
- 1 recipe Ginger Salad Dressing
- ⅓ cup chopped peanuts

curried chicken salad

Ladies' luncheons have changed and so has chicken salad. Today's version is a riot of color—red grapes, green celery, orange slices—and looks to the East for its flavorings of soy sauce and curry.

84

- 2 medium oranges or one 11-ounce can mandarin orange sections, drained
- 3 cups cubed cooked chicken (about 1 pound)
- 2 cups seedless red grapes, halved
- 1 8-ounce can sliced water chestnuts, drained
- 1 cup thinly sliced celery
- ⅓ cup light mayonnaise dressing or salad dressing
- ⅓ cup lemon-flavored low-fat yogurt
- 2 teaspoons soy sauce
- 1 teaspoon curry powder

Prep: 30 minutes   Chill: 4 to 24 hours   Makes 6 servings

If using fresh oranges, peel and slice; halve or quarter each slice. In a large mixing bowl combine oranges, chicken, grapes, water chestnuts, and celery.

For dressing, in a small bowl stir together light mayonnaise dressing, yogurt, soy sauce, and curry powder. Pour dressing over chicken mixture; toss lightly to coat. Cover and chill for 4 to 24 hours.

Nutrition facts per serving: 275 cal., 11 g total fat (3 g sat. fat), 68 mg chol., 299 mg sodium, 22 g carbo., 2 g fiber, 24 g pro. Daily values: 2% vit. A, 50% vit. C, 5% calcium, 10% iron

italian zucchini salad

Ever seen the beautiful layered vegetables in glass jars sitting on counters at Italian groceries? Bring those artful creations to mind with this striking mixture of vegetables, beans, and prosciutto, bound together with a creamy dressing.

86

2 large zucchini and/or yellow summer squash, cut into ¼-inch-thick slices (4 cups)

1 15½-ounce can white kidney beans, rinsed and drained

1 7¼-ounce jar roasted red sweet peppers, drained and cut into thin strips

4 ounces prosciutto, cut into thin strips (1 cup)

6 cups torn fresh spinach

2 cups torn arugula

⅓ cup bottled creamy Italian salad dressing

¼ cup light mayonnaise dressing or salad dressing

1 cup shredded provolone or fontina cheese (4 ounces)

½ cup Italian parsley leaves

Prep: 30 minutes   Chill: 2 to 24 hours   Makes 8 servings

In a large bowl combine zucchini, beans, roasted red pepper strips, and prosciutto. Cover and chill for 2 to 24 hours.

Just before serving, add spinach and arugula to zucchini mixture; toss to combine.

For dressing, stir together Italian salad dressing and light mayonnaise dressing; pour over zucchini mixture. Toss lightly to coat. Add shredded cheese and parsley; toss to combine.

Nutrition facts per serving: 221 cal., 15 g total fat (4 g sat. fat), 10 mg chol., 628 mg sodium, 14 g carbo., 5 g fiber, 12 g pro. Daily values: 46% vit. A, 122% vit. C, 15% calcium, 16% iron

boston bean salad with ham

A mixture of glistening high-contrast beans can look glamorous set off by rings of green onion and pink cubes of ham. The taste recalls time-honored Yankee bean-pot dishes, but the fast prep time puts it squarely in the moment.

Prep: 20 minutes   Chill: 4 to 24 hours   Makes 8 servings

In a large bowl combine desired beans, celery, and green onions.

For dressing, whisk together the vinegar, molasses, oil, and mustard. Pour dressing over bean mixture; toss lightly to coat. Cover and chill for 4 to 24 hours, stirring occasionally.

To serve, line a salad bowl or platter with lettuce. Stir ham into bean mixture. Using a slotted spoon, transfer bean mixture to lettuce-lined salad bowl or platter.

Nutrition facts per serving: 311 cal., 10 g total fat (2 g sat. fat), 19 mg chol., 1,144 mg sodium, 39 g carbo., 7 g fiber, 19 g pro. Daily values: 2% vit. A, 18% vit. C, 8% calcium, 26% iron

3   15-ounce cans desired beans, such as navy beans, red kidney beans, or black beans, rinsed and drained

1   cup sliced celery

½   cup thinly sliced green onions

½   cup vinegar

¼   cup molasses

¼   cup salad oil

1   tablespoon Dijon-style mustard

    Lettuce leaves

2   cups chopped cooked ham (10 ounces)

red beans & grains

Eliminate the serving dish by using a crusty round of hearth-baked bread for a salad bowl. Inside are red beans, ham, and quinoa—a bead-shape grain that's loaded with protein. Brown rice can substitute for the quinoa.

Prep: 30 minutes   Chill: 2 to 24 hours   Makes 10 to 12 servings

In a large bowl combine ham, quinoa, beans, white rice, tomato, sweet pepper, green onions, parsley, and jalapeño pepper. Pour vinaigrette over rice mixture; toss lightly to coat. Cover and chill for 2 to 24 hours.

Just before serving, cut a 1-inch slice from the top of each loaf of bread. Hollow out bread, leaving a ¼- to ½-inch-thick shell. (Save top slice and remaining bread for another use.) Line each of the bread bowls with lettuce. Spoon salad into bread bowls.

Peppered Vinaigrette: In a screw-top jar combine 3 tablespoons olive oil; 3 tablespoons red wine vinegar; 2 cloves garlic, minced; 2 teaspoons snipped fresh thyme or ½ teaspoon dried thyme, crushed; ½ teaspoon ground black pepper; and ¼ teaspoon ground red pepper. Cover and shake well.

Nutrition facts per serving: 333 cal., 9 g total fat (2 g sat. fat), 24 mg chol., 961 mg sodium, 45 g carbo., 5 g fiber, 18 g pro. Daily values: 4% vit. A, 66% vit. C, 7% calcium, 29% iron

- 3 cups diced cooked ham (about 1 pound)
- 2 cups cooked quinoa or brown rice
- 1 15-ounce can pinto beans, rinsed and drained
- 1 cup cooked white rice
- 1 large tomato, chopped (1 cup)
- 1 yellow or green sweet pepper, chopped (¾ cup)
- ¼ cup thinly sliced green onions
- ¼ cup snipped fresh parsley
- 1 jalapeño pepper, finely chopped
- 1 recipe Peppered Vinaigrette
- 3 8-inch round loaves crusty bread (country bread)

  Red-tip leaf lettuce

muffuletta salad

Bring a bit of New Orleans to any gathering with this do-ahead salad that serves a dozen hungry eaters. The salami, ham, cheese, broccoli, and tomatoes are layered and chilled, then topped with toasted bread cubes, recalling the famed muffuletta sandwiches.

90

- 4 1-inch-thick slices Italian bread
- 2 tablespoons bottled Italian salad dressing or olive oil
- 1 medium red sweet pepper, cut into strips
- ¾ cup bottled Italian salad dressing
- ½ cup sliced celery
- ½ cup sliced pitted green or ripe olives
- 3 tablespoons snipped fresh basil or oregano
- 6 to 8 cups torn romaine
- ½ pound salami, cut into bite-size strips
- ½ pound lean cooked ham, cut into bite-size strips
- 8 ounces cubed provolone cheese
- 1½ cups broccoli flowerets
- 1½ cups cherry tomatoes, halved

Prep: 30 minutes   Chill: 4 to 24 hours   Makes 12 servings

For croutons, brush Italian bread slices with the 2 tablespoons salad dressing. Cut into 1-inch cubes. Spread in a large shallow baking pan. Bake in a 300° oven about 15 minutes or until crisp, stirring once or twice. Cool. Store in an airtight container.

Meanwhile, in a very large bowl combine sweet pepper strips, the ¾ cup salad dressing, celery, olives, and basil. Layer in the following order: romaine, salami, ham, cheese, broccoli, and cherry tomatoes. Cover and chill for 4 to 24 hours.

Just before serving, add croutons to salad; toss lightly to coat.

Nutrition facts per serving: 299 cal., 22 g total fat (7 g sat. fat), 38 mg chol., 1,133 mg sodium, 11 g carbo., 2 g fiber, 15 g pro. Daily values: 22% vit. A, 63% vit. C, 14% calcium, 10% iron

two-bean & rice salad

When you need to feed a crowd, consider this pleaser that easily can be doubled to serve 30. Pinto beans and black beans provide color contrast, and garlic dressing and diced chili peppers give it verve.

Prep: 25 minutes   Chill: 2 to 24 hours   Makes 16 servings

In a large mixing bowl combine rice, beans, peas, celery, onion, peppers, and cilantro.

Pour dressing over the rice mixture; toss lightly to coat. Cover and chill for 2 to 24 hours.

Garlic Dressing: In a screw-top jar combine $\frac{1}{3}$ cup white wine vinegar, $\frac{1}{4}$ cup olive oil or salad oil, 2 tablespoons water, $\frac{3}{4}$ teaspoon salt, $\frac{1}{2}$ teaspoon garlic powder, and $\frac{1}{2}$ teaspoon pepper. Cover and shake well.

Nutrition facts per serving: 244 cal., 7 g total fat (1 g sat. fat), 0 mg chol., 591 mg sodium, 39 g carbo., 7 g fiber, 9 g pro. Daily values: 2% vit. A, 27% vit. C, 5% calcium, 19% iron

3 cups cooked rice, chilled

1 15-ounce can pinto beans, rinsed and drained

1 15-ounce can black beans, rinsed and drained

1 10-ounce package frozen peas, thawed

1 cup sliced celery

$\frac{1}{2}$ cup chopped red onion

2 medium fresh Anaheim peppers, chopped, or two 4-ounce cans diced green chili peppers, drained

$\frac{1}{4}$ cup snipped fresh cilantro or parsley

1 recipe Garlic Dressing or $\frac{2}{3}$ cup bottled Italian salad dressing

three-cheese orzo salad

Orzo is pasta shaped like rice that cooks in less than 10 minutes. It's a useful base for vegetables, and, like all pastas, was born to be served with cheese. Make it a triple indulgence with feta, mozzarella, and Parmesan.

92

2 cups sugar snap peas, ends trimmed

1¼ cups orzo

1 6-ounce jar marinated artichoke hearts

2 cups red or yellow cherry tomatoes and/or baby pear tomatoes, halved

1 cup cubed mozzarella cheese (4 ounces)

1 4-ounce package crumbled feta or peppercorn feta cheese (1 cup)

¼ cup shredded Parmesan cheese (1 ounce)

¼ cup white wine vinegar

¼ cup water

2 teaspoons sugar

1 tablespoon snipped fresh dill or 1 teaspoon dried dillweed

Prep: 30 minutes   Chill: 4 to 24 hours   Makes 8 servings

Cook sugar snap peas in a large saucepan of boiling, lightly salted water for 1 minute. Using a slotted spoon, transfer peas to a colander. Rinse under cold water; drain and set aside.

Add orzo to the same saucepan. Boil for 8 to 10 minutes or until tender but firm; drain. Rinse with cold water; drain again.

Meanwhile, drain artichoke hearts, reserving marinade. Cut artichokes into bite-size pieces. In a large bowl toss together artichokes, sugar snap peas, orzo, tomatoes, and cheeses.

For dressing, in a screw-top jar combine reserved artichoke marinade, vinegar, water, sugar, and dill. Cover and shake well. Pour dressing over salad. Toss lightly to coat. Cover and chill for 4 to 24 hours.

Nutrition facts per serving: 233 cal., 8 g total fat (4 g sat. fat), 23 mg chol., 336 mg sodium, 28 g carbo., 1 g fiber, 12 g pro. Daily values: 9% vit. A, 38% vit. C, 17% calcium, 13% iron

By making a few conversions, cooks in Australia, Canada, and the United Kingdom can use the recipes in *Better Homes and Gardens*® *Fresh and Simple*™ *Quick-Toss Salad Meals* with confidence. The charts on this page provide a guide for converting measurements from the U.S. customary system, which is used throughout this book, to the imperial and metric systems. There also is a conversion table for oven temperatures to accommodate the differences in oven calibrations.

Product Differences: Most of the ingredients called for in the recipes in this book are available in English-speaking countries. However, some are known by different names. Here are some common American ingredients and their possible counterparts:

- Sugar is granulated or castor sugar.
- Powdered sugar is icing sugar.
- All-purpose flour is plain household flour or white flour. When self-rising flour is used in place of all-purpose flour in a recipe that calls for leavening, omit the leavening agent (baking soda or baking powder) and salt.
- Light-colored corn syrup is golden syrup.
- Cornstarch is cornflour.
- Baking soda is bicarbonate of soda.
- Vanilla is vanilla essence.
- Green, red, or yellow sweet peppers are capsicums.
- Golden raisins are sultanas.

Volume and Weight: Americans traditionally use cup measures for liquid and solid ingredients. The chart, above right, shows the approximate imperial and metric equivalents. If you are accustomed to weighing solid ingredients, the following approximate equivalents will be helpful.

- 1 cup butter, castor sugar, or rice = 8 ounces = about 250 grams
- 1 cup flour = 4 ounces = about 125 grams
- 1 cup icing sugar = 5 ounces = about 150 grams

Spoon measures are used for smaller amounts of ingredients. Although the size of the tablespoon varies slightly in different countries, for practical purposes and for recipes in this book, a straight substitution is all that's necessary.

Measurements made using cups or spoons always should be level unless stated otherwise.

Equivalents: U.S. = Australia/U.K.

⅛ teaspoon = 0.5 ml
¼ teaspoon = 1 ml
½ teaspoon = 2 ml
1 teaspoon = 5 ml
1 tablespoon = 1 tablespoon
¼ cup = 2 tablespoons = 2 fluid ounces = 60 ml
⅓ cup = ¼ cup = 3 fluid ounces = 90 ml
½ cup = ⅓ cup = 4 fluid ounces = 120 ml
⅔ cup = ½ cup = 5 fluid ounces = 150 ml
¾ cup = ⅔ cup = 6 fluid ounces = 180 ml
1 cup = ¾ cup = 8 fluid ounces = 240 ml
1¼ cups = 1 cup
2 cups = 1 pint
1 quart = 1 liter
½ inch = 1.27 cm
1 inch = 2.54 cm

Baking Pan Sizes

American	Metric
8×1½-inch round baking pan	20×4-cm cake tin
9×1½-inch round baking pan	23×3.5-cm cake tin
11×7×1½-inch baking pan	28×18×4-cm baking tin
13×9×2-inch baking pan	30×20×3-cm baking tin
2-quart rectangular baking dish	30×20×3-cm baking tin
15×10×1-inch baking pan	30×25×2-cm baking tin (Swiss roll tin)
9-inch pie plate	22×4- or 23×4-cm pie plate
7- or 8-inch springform pan	18- or 20-cm springform or loose-bottom cake tin
9×5×3-inch loaf pan	23×13×7-cm or 2-pound narrow loaf tin or pâté tin
1½-quart casserole	1.5-liter casserole
2-quart casserole	2-liter casserole

Oven Temperature Equivalents

Fahrenheit Setting	Celsius Setting*	Gas Setting
300°F	150°C	Gas Mark 2 (slow)
325°F	160°C	Gas Mark 3 (moderately slow)
350°F	180°C	Gas Mark 4 (moderate)
375°F	190°C	Gas Mark 5 (moderately hot)
400°F	200°C	Gas Mark 6 (hot)
425°F	220°C	Gas Mark 7
450°F	230°C	Gas Mark 8 (very hot)
Broil		Grill

Electric and gas ovens may be calibrated using Celsius. However, for an electric oven, increase the Celsius setting 10 to 20 degrees when cooking above 160°C. For convection or forced-air ovens (gas or electric), lower the temperature setting 10°C when cooking at all heat levels.